ALLEG HV854.D73 1983
Dreskin, William.
The day care decision

3036000000280943

D1786628

HV 854 .D73 1983
Dreskin, William.
The day care decision.

DATE DUE

DE 8 '88	JUN 2 2 1992	
AP 21 '89		
OC 26 '89		
NO 29 '89	MAR 2 4 1993	
APR 11 1990	APR 1 6 1993	
OC 17 '90	NOV 1 1994	
DE 10 '90		
NOV 20 1991		
APR 11 1992	NOV 1 7 1994	
MAY 0 6 1992	DEC 6 1994	
	DEC 15 1994	

MAR 3 1 1998

APR 28 1999

THE COMMUNITY COLLEGE OF ALLEGHENY COUNTY
ALLEGHENY CAMPUS
808 RIDGE AVENUE
PITTSBURGH, PA.
15212
LIBRARY

DEMCO

The Day Care Decision

The Day Care Decision

What's Best for You and Your Child

by William Dreskin
and Wendy Dreskin

M. Evans and Company, Inc.
New York

Lyrics from the following songs appear as epigraphs in Chapter 8, "Pressures on Child Raisers," by permission of the copyright holders.

"Mayn Yingele" translated by Ruth Rubin. © 1964 by Appleseed Music, Inc.

"I Am a Rock" by Paul Simon. Copyright © 1965 Paul Simon.

Library of Congress Cataloging in Publication Data

Dreskin, William.
   The day care decision.

   Bibliography: p.
   Includes index.
   1. Day care centers—United States. 2. Child development—United States. 3. Parent and child—United States. I. Dreskin, Wendy. II. Title.
HV854.D73   1983   362.7'12   83-16483

ISBN 0-87131-418-5

Copyright © 1983 by William Dreskin and Wendy Dreskin

All rights reserved. No part of this book may be reproduced or transmitted in any form or by any means without the written permission of the publisher.

M. Evans and Company, Inc.
216 East 49 Street
New York, New York 10017

Design by Nancy Sugihara
Manufactured in the United States of America

9 8 7 6 5 4 3 2 1

*To our daughter, Tanya,
and to children everywhere*

Contents

Foreword 8
Preface 10
Acknowledgments 13

Part One · The Child's World

1 The Early Years: Your Child's Emotional Development 17

Closeness, Caring and Your Child • Day Care's Effect on Emotional Development • Types f Substitute Care • Day Care and Children with Special Needs • The Parent's Role

2 The Day Care Debate 32

Studying Attachment: Problems and Perils • Availability of Information

3 Inside Day Care: A Child's-Eye View 44

Inside Day Care • Our Decision

4 Tuning In: Becoming More Sensitive to Your Child's Needs 60

Day Care: How We Got Here • A Stranger in Our Midst • Kids Are People Too

5 Health and Your Child   68

Warning: Day Care May Be Hazardous to Your Child's Health • Exposure to Infection Is Not Beneficial • The Day Care Center: Pressures Against Health

6 Early Childhood Education   81

The Development of Early Childhood Education • Play and "Serious Learning" • More Is Not Better • Learning and the Whole Chi

7 What's Best for Your Child   92

Part Two · The Parents' View

8 Pressures on Child Raisers   97

Pressures on Fathers • Flight from Intimacy

9 Pressures on Mothers   106

Women's Liberation • Tinker, Tailor, Soldier, Sailor, Housewife • The Grass Is Greener: The Myth of the Happy Worker • The Supermom • Children Are the Future Society

10 Overcoming Doubts About Being a Child Raiser   120

Loneliness and Isolation • Boredom and Bananas • "I'm Not Cut Out for This" • Mush Brain • What Do You Do, Mommy? • Am I Wasting My Talents? • Don't Be a Block Mother Unless You Want to Be • Is Mothering Being Overprotective? • Financial Pressures • Reentry

Part Three · The Family Here and Abroad

11 Solutions in Other Countries: Help for Child Raisers and Working Parents   137

The Solution: More Choices • Child Care and the Welfare State • Help for Full-Time Child Raisers • Help for Working Parents

12 Solutions in the United States   148
   New Options for Workers • New Options for Fathers

13 Personal Solutions   156
   The Child at Home • The Child in the Workplace

14 The Future for the Working Parent: Choices and Changes   171
   The Computer: Redefining the Workplace • Trends in Employment • Family Advocacy • Some Concluding Thoughts

Appendix I: The "Day Care Diseases"   180

Appendix II: National Job Sharing Network Members   183

Suggested Reading   185

Index   187

Foreword

The single most inflammatory topic having to do with young children today is the issue of full-time substitute care for infants. Interestingly, the topic is more inflammatory among professionals (in my opinion) than it is among parents. Parents are concerned. Indeed, many of them are either carrying a huge load of guilt because they are using substitute care for babies as young as two or three months of age, or they are feeling a good deal of pressure because they are not using such care and they are hearing messages to the effect that they are not doing enough with their lives. Ironically, feelings are running very high among interested people, even though all parties concerned are invariably decent, caring people.

Five or six outstanding books on the subject of substitute care have been published recently. In addition, over the last four or five years the subject has been treated extensively in magazines, especially those addressed to young women.

This new book by William and Wendy Dreskin, *The Day Care Decision: What's Best for You and Your Child,* is unique. The Dreskins bring to this important topic a perspective of people who not only have been professionally involved in early childhood education for some time, but also have participated in the recent evolution leading to the popularity of substitute care. They modified their nursery school to become a provider of substitute care as well as early childhood education. After almost two years of such experience, they found themselves so uncomfortable that they felt they could not continue to offer that kind of service and, furthermore, they became highly motivated to write about the issues. The result is this book—a book written by warm, thoughtful practitioners, a book that is clearly a product of passion and deep concern.

Its primary messages are that full-time substitute care for children under three is rarely advisable (except in cases of extreme hardship) and that the people who choose to be full-time child rearers of their own children deserve full support, because what they are involved in is at least as important as anything else they might be doing. In addition, they make a very strong case for increased involvement of men in the parenting process.

Having run a day care operation, they are in a much better position than many commentators on this subject to talk about the nuts and bolts of such activities. The examples taken from their own journals are telling, although admittedly somewhat dramatic on occasion. The information on the health hazards due to the spread of contagious diseases and on policies of European countries is to the point and most valuable.

In all, their message is quite similar to my own, which has come from a very lengthy period of research on what's best for young children. While some of their reasons for their recommendations are quite different from mine, the conclusions show almost total overlap. This book brings to the debate about whether to use full-time substitute care for infants considerable thoughtfulness about the impact on the child, and helps correct the current imbalance of emphasis on the needs of the parents. I recommend it strongly.

BURTON L. WHITE
Center for Parent Education
Newton, Massachusetts

Preface

We feel a brief explanation of how we came to write this book is in order. It is unlikely that this book would ever have been written if we had not been directors of a day care center. But in the beginning, we did not offer day care; that came later.

In California in 1973, we founded a nonprofit preschool for three- to five-year-olds because we were very interested in early childhood education, and because we were idealistic about improving society. We were fascinated by the openness and honesty of very young children, and believed that through working with young children society could be transformed from the inside. We both had teaching credentials, and Wendy had worked with small groups of preschool children in informal settings for several years prior to opening the school.

After operating a successful half-day preschool program for three years, we were confident that at least some of our goals were being accomplished. Our well-equipped facility with a qualified staff created an educational, rather than custodial, situation, and the children were blossoming with the individual attention they received. But more and more mothers were going back to work and could not take advantage of a morning preschool. As rent and other expenses went up, it became increasingly difficult to make ends meet with the facility in use only three hours a day. We decided to open the school up for full-time day care for three- to five-year-olds, and before- and after-school care for children in kindergarten through third grade. We had run a good preschool, and we were sure our training, our idealism, and our love of children would enable us to run a good day care center.

We knew that many programs were mainly custodial, with such a high ratio of children to adults that individual attention was neglected. We were also aware of the extreme end of the spectrum:

poorly run, poorly equipped day care programs. Stories of severe neglect and abuse in day care homes and day care centers were very disturbing to us. The horrors of mental, physical, and emotional deprivation were etched in our minds. But we were going to offer a quality day care program. We did not have the slightest suspicion that there might be a serious problem with even the best day care programs.

Seeing the entire period of change, we had a very good basis for comparison. We saw the clientele change from parents who cared about their children's educational development to parents who wanted a custodial arrangement. Harried parents who wanted day care rarely were interested in seeing our brochure and other handouts describing the program, and seldom asked to observe at the center. They simply asked the hours and the cost before enrolling. Parent meetings went from nearly 100 percent attendance to such poor attendance that we gave up holding them. The education books in our lending library just sat on the shelf, except when a college student teacher or high-school work-experience student checked them out.

We also saw some of the same boys and girls we had known as preschoolers (children who attended the program from 9:00 A.M. to noon) become different children when they were subjected to the stress of full-time day care. We saw the differences between the children who still came for only half a day for preschool and the children who attended full time.

After a year and a half of seeing this, we could no longer bear to watch. It was obvious that the children did not feel that staff-given understanding and comforting were adequate compensation for spending forty or fifty hours a week away from their parents. We found ourselves talking the center out of business, telling parents inquiring about the program that they should try if possible to work part time until the children were older.

We did no tests on the children at the center. We listened to them, played with them, held them, watched them, taught them—and we did not need an instrument to measure the negative effects long separation from their parents had on them.

As we became concerned about the day care children in our own center, we began to talk to other day care directors, day care workers, and parents who had children in day care at other centers; the quotations in the following chapters are taken from these and other interviews. We began to read studies about the effects of day care on young children, and came to realize how difficult it is to scientifically research the effects of this experiment in child raising that we call day care. But we felt we had an obligation to the unhappy day care children at our center, and to all children in day care, to find out why, with the best intentions, we couldn't "replace" these children's parents on a daily basis. We hope this book is a step toward answering this crucial question, and will be useful to parents wondering if, when, how much, and what kind of day care is best for their child.

Acknowledgments

Many parents across the country gladly shared the joys and frustrations of child raising with us. We would especially like to thank Linda Aiello, Patricia and William Freiert, Angela Gonsman, Susan Hansbury, Jerrold and Robin Kaufman, Joann Manning, Liba and Karel Placek, Linda Scobey, and Susan Silverstein. We would also like to thank Dr. Gregor Katz for his insights, as a grandfather and a child psychiatrist, into family life in Sweden.

For his generous assistance, we thank Dr. Stephen Hadler at the Centers for Disease Control. His careful review of Chapter 5 and corrections for accuracy were invaluable.

We thank Ruth Rubin for permission to use her poignant translation of the sweatshop worker's song, and Judith Nolte at *American Baby* for permission to quote from her editorial and from the "Letters to the Editor."

The subject of day care and its effects on emotional development is a complex one. We would like to thank Dr. Burton White for his expert advice and guidance.

Much thanks to Leon Dreskin for his enthusiasm and encouragement on this project from its conception to the completion of the book.

Finally, we thank Herb Katz at M. Evans and Company for realizing the urgency of this issue, and Linda Cabasin for her enthusiasm and editorial guidance.

PART ONE
The Child's World

Chapter One

The Early Years: Your Child's Emotional Development

The family experience is being diluted and diminished by the increasing use of full-time day care for young children. Most parents realize that the decision whether to put their child in someone else's care, and the choice as to the kind of arrangement, will significantly affect their work and family life. But very few are aware of how full-time day care affects their child's life, and the effects of the extensive use of full-time day care on the nature and direction of our whole society are not readily discernible.

The United States is one of the few industrialized nations that does not provide a child care leave. Mothers are expected to return to work as soon as they are physically able to do so, typically after a six-week disability leave. While the future holds the prospect of more choices for the American working parent, the current climate frequently pushes parents into unhappy compromises and second-best situations.

The years before school age pass very rapidly and are irretrievable for both parents and children. Parents try to balance priorities, and may decide to take an extended leave or quit their job, or choose to work part-time and avoid putting their children in full-time day care. Some will decide that they cannot afford even that compromise. But virtually all parents making the day care decision lack vital information necessary to make an informed choice. It is essential that parents understand exactly what the family setting provides for their child, physically and emotionally, and that they recognize the abilities and limitations of full-time day care to adequately fill their child's needs.

Closeness, Caring, and Your Child

Full-time day care, particularly group care, is not an adequate substitute for time spent with parents, and can be especially harmful for children under the age of three. For two years we watched day care children in our preschool/day care center respond to the stresses of eight to ten hours a day of separation from their parents with tears, anger, withdrawal, or profound sadness, and we found, to our dismay, that nothing in our own affection and caring for these children would erase this sense of loss and abandonment. We came to realize that the amount of separation—the number of hours a day spent away from the parents—is a critical factor.

Before discussing the problems of full-time substitute care and its effect on children's emotional development, we will examine children's need for love and attention, closeness and caring, at various stages of development. The issue of full-time separation makes it necessary to look carefully at the roots of a child's feelings for the parent and the parent's feelings of love for the child. The problem of substitute care can be appreciated only in the context of understanding the essential role of parents in children's emotional development.

Young children have needs beyond food and warmth; they need to have an intimate emotional relationship. And parents put a great deal of energy into loving and caring for their child. There are rewards, but what defines the love parents feel is that they continue to care for the baby even when great effort and patience are required. If there is love, a father does not put his infant up for adoption because he was up crying eight times in one night. A mother does not stop loving her toddler even though she has just pulled the tablecloth off and broken the best china. Parents will, of course, feel frustrated and angry from time to time. But parents do not say, "I'll support you for eighteen years if you'll support me in my old age." They can love a mentally or physically handicapped baby whom they may have to support for a lifetime, and deeply care for a child whose life will most definitely be cut short by a terminal illness. In other words, parents are willing to give of themselves without any condition, without any thought of immediately receiving something in return. When a person chooses to relate in that way to a baby (or to another adult, for that matter), we call that deep caring love.

From the child's point of view, this kind of active caring and attention given by the parent produces feelings of security and intense happiness; the child forms a specific attachment with strong feelings of love toward the parent or parents. The word *parent* here refers to anyone who is a primary attachment for the young child. When a child develops deep feelings of love toward a specific adult through a constant and sustained relationship, then that adult is a psychological parent to the child, even if he or she is not the biological parent.

It is important to understand that a young child's attachment to a parent—sometimes called bonding—occurs over a period of several years and is an enormously complex and constantly changing process. And, of course, the parent's way of responding also changes through the stages of this development. By the age of eight weeks the baby can smile in response to a human face, and between the ages of six weeks and eight months the baby's attachment to the parent/care giver grows so that by the eighth to twelfth month the baby responds to separation from the parent with distress, and shows signs of grieving if the separation is lengthy. Some tolerance for separation from the parent(s) gradually develops between one and two and a half years of age, and this capacity for longer and longer separations free of trauma continues to develop from two and a half through kindergarten.

Studies and observations of children's behavior from birth through the preschool years (up to five) do not give detailed information about children's feelings of attachment for their parents. (The terms *attachment* and *bond* are used interchangeably in this book.) To really understand this special feeling and special relationship we must turn to child psychiatry and psychoanalysis, with their exploration of the inner thoughts and feelings of children at different stages of development. Most child psychiatrists and child psychologists agree that young children, including newborns and infants, are affected by the nature, quantity, and quality of the care they receive. It is generally recognized that young children must form a close attachment with a parent or parents and receive consistent caring and affection if they are to avoid deficits or disturbances in their emotional development.

The late Selma Fraiberg, in *Every Child's Birthright* (Basic Books, 1977), notes that parents' intuitive sense of the importance of a close attachment with their child is quite valid. " 'Mothering,' that old-fashioned word, is the nurturing of the human potential of every baby to love, trust, and to bind himself to human partnerships in a lifetime of love." She cites studies in animal behavior that show that this need for emotional as well as physical nurturing is not unique to humans. Having physical needs met does not prevent the abnormal behavior many young animals display when deprived of contact with the mother.

Dr. Benjamin Spock, in *Raising Children in a Difficult Time* (W. W. Norton, 1974), concurs that the first years are critical in children's emotional development. He notes that psychological and psychoanalytical studies "all agree that the first two or three years are the most crucial ones." And Dr. Burton White, regarded as the foremost authority on the optimal educational development of infants and toddlers, and author of *The First Three Years of Life* (Prentice-Hall, 1975), also asserts that studies in human development demonstrate the central importance of the first years in the emotional development of children.

During this critical formative period the child has a need to form a close attachment with a particular parent, and this is achieved through frequent physical contact, verbal and nonverbal interaction, and the development of a sense of trust. The parent must consistently and reliably respond to the child's demand for attention, or this sense of trust will not be established. The parent's contacts with the child must be frequent and sustained in the first years if the relationship is to have depth and a special meaning for the child. The amount of contact time needed is less and less as the child matures. Dr. White believes—and the authors' experience and observations bear this out—that a half-day contact is quite adequate by the time the child reaches three.

The two essential ingredients in this primary attachment of the child to the parent are specificity and constancy. It is the presence of these two factors that allows bonding to take place. Simply put, the child must continually relate to that particular person, and this relationship must continue over several years if the child is to have an overall experience of contentment and emotional well-being.

The similarity of children's love relationships with their parents and adult love relationships, which also require specificity and constancy, is not coincidental. Psychoanalytical investigations show that children's attachment to their parents in the early years is the foundation and wellspring of adult love. The intensity and idealization of romantic love have their source in the child's idealization of the parent, the first intense love relationship with another human being. As Fraiberg notes, in the work cited, the adult love relationship "has its origin in the discovery of the first human partner in infancy."

What happens to a child who, for one reason or another, does not have the opportunity to form a close attachment in the first years; who is deprived of this experience of mutual love and caring in this critical developmental period? For obvious reasons, researchers have not experimentally created emotional-deprivation situations for human infants in order to study the effects, but "natural" situations such as war have provided an opportunity for child psychiatrists, child psychoanalysts, and pediatricians to study extreme cases of "maternal deprivation" as it is called, where the children—war orphans, for example—did not have the benefit of a sustained close attachment with a parent.

It is not surprising that these extreme situations produced severe and easily measurable damage. René Spitz's studies (1945) of infants in an orphanage found that babies deprived of close contact with an adult deteriorated mentally to the point where, at the age of two, they would not respond to the sight of a human. It was found that these severely deprived infants who had only the most superficial and transient contact with adult care givers could not form a close attachment when they were later adopted into a loving environment. Long-term studies of infants and children who experienced severe maternal deprivation confirm the suspicion that as adults they experience marked emotional difficulties. In Sally Provence and Rose Lipton's study of deprivation, *Infants in Institutions* (International Universities Press, 1962), gross long-lasting deficiencies in all areas of development, including the capacity to form close attachments, were found in spite of the fact that this institutional setting was far superior to the orphanage in the Spitz study. Studies of children raised in foster homes reveal similar problems, so that it is clear that nonattachment or disrupted attachment, particularly during the first two or three years of life, can produce retarded development and emotional deficits.

Reports that nonorphaned round-the-clock day care children in the Eastern Bloc countries showed signs of deprivation suggest that the amount of separation from parents can be a critical factor. These children, who stayed at the day care centers from Monday morning until Friday night, were unable to laugh and showed other signs of deprivation. This occurred despite the fact that in some countries, such as Czechoslovakia, they had been placed in day care only after an initial six-month child care leave. Six months with their mother and time with their parents on weekends was not sufficient to protect these young children from the effects of maternal deprivation.

As we said previously, the essential aspects of a child's attachment to a parent are specificity and constancy, and it is clear that the orphanage or foster home situation can interfere with both of these factors. But one very interesting fact that emerges from studies such as these is that the degree of damage is variable and is roughly proportional to the degree of deprivation. This corresponds to our common-sense notion of human attachments and emotional needs. The requirements of specificity and constancy can be satisfied to varying degrees. To put it in less scientific terms, a child can feel all degrees of closeness or attachment toward the parent, just as there are varying degrees of closeness in all kinds of relationships.

This point is central in the following discussion of why full-time substitute care interferes with young children's forming a close loving relationship with their parents in the first years. There is a vast emotional spectrum between the inferior-quality orphanage and severely disturbed family at one end of the scale and the child's close attachment in a loving family environment on the other. The day care debate, which is discussed in Chapter 2, rests on the issue of where forty or fifty hours a week of separation from the parents for different-aged children falls in this scale. It is sufficient to note here that the determination of the exact number of hours per day that parents should spend with their children in the earliest years in order to ensure the formation of a close bond and close relationship is currently beyond the scope of psychological studies and experiments. But, as Dr. Burton White pointed out in an interview with the authors, perhaps, in discussing substitute care and children's emotional needs, parents should think in terms of what is optimal for their child's emotional development rather than what is the absolute minimum requirement in order to avoid damage.

Day Care's Effect on Emotional Development

In looking at the effect of various kinds of day care arrangements on children's emotional development, parents must consider two different issues. First, in terms of a child's need for a close attachment, is there a substitute? Would, for example, many casual relationships with adults somehow "add up" to the emotional equivalent of a close loving relationship with a parent? (Here again we use the word *parent* in the psychological, not biological, sense.) Second, can lengthy separation from the parents dilute or block the process of bonding with them? How much time should parents spend with their children to ensure that a close relationship is established?

Unfortunately, there is no simple answer to either question, since the answers depend on the age and stage of development of the child and the length and type of substitute care. Nevertheless, meaningful generalizations can be made as long as the age factor and type of care are taken into consideration. (See also Chapter 7.)

Parents facing the day care decision can begin to find answers to these questions by thinking about adult love relationships. As discussed in the first section, psychoanalytical investigations have shown that adults' love relationships are strikingly similar to and derive from the love relationships with their parents in early childhood. They provide a good model to test out some of these ideas. We will discuss the issues of substitute care and length of separation together, since they are almost always two sides of the same coin in actual family situations.

We frequently use the term *emotional bond*, but this can be very misleading. It makes it sound as though at birth the child forms an immediate attachment to the parent and that's it. Dr. Marshall Klaus and Dr. John Kennell write in *Parent-Infant Bonding* (The C. V. Mosby Company, 1982), "Some misinterpretation of studies in this area may have resulted from a too literal acceptance of the word *bonding* and so has suggested that the speed of this reaction resembles the epoxy bonding of materials." For an initial emotional bond to meet the child's needs, it must involve a sustained relationship with the parent. Just as the lungs need a constantly renewed supply of oxygen, children and adults have certain emotional needs that cannot be filled by a single dose, however large. Imagine a couple completing a wonderful honeymoon by kissing and saying good-bye. They won't be seeing each other anymore because they have formed an attachment; their emotional needs have been satisfied. Obviously, availability and continuity are important elements. A husband and wife may be unhappy because they are not getting to spend enough time together, even though they know—as a child may not know—that love and firm commitment are there.

"A day care worker can enhance the mother-child bond," claims one day care director we interviewed. "The day care worker can tell the mother when she picks up her child in the evening, 'He really liked his string beans today,' or 'He crawled this far.'" This might make the parent feel better about the long separation, but it is not relevant to the child's feelings. We interviewed Dr. Phyllis Levenstein, a keen observer of child development and a professor at State University of New York, who said, "Bonding comes about because of a *direct* relationship between a parent and child. It cannot happen via a third person."

A young child's emotional needs for closeness and caring cannot be met by an attachment unless that attachment is followed by a long process of relating in which the parent is physically and emotionally available to the child. As the child matures, longer and longer periods of separation become acceptable. Preschoolers and kindergartners are like underwater swimmers who find they can go for increasingly longer distances before they have to return to the surface.

Group care at an early age dilutes or interrupts bonding to the parent without offering the possibility of an attachment to a surrogate parent. It is very likely that for infants and toddlers the interruption of this early process results in a long-standing emotional deficit.

Between the ages of three and five, children who are already attached to a parent continue the bonding process, but they become more and more independent. If they have had adequate nurturing for three years or more, an interruption in the process at this time will produce feelings of longing, sadness, or anger, but it is unlikely to result in significant long-standing damage. As the deprivation studies show, there is something inherent in the development of children in the earliest years that makes adequate nurturing at that point critical. A close relationship fortifies children for the future. Once established, it cannot be easily undone.

Some day care advocates argue that less attachment in the early years will be beneficial to the child and make the child stronger and more independent. This is an adult perspective. It is true that some adults feel more "independent" when they do not have the vulnerability of a close relationship or commitment. But for the young child it is better to have loved and lost than never to have loved at all. Most psychologists and psychoanalysts agree that a nonattached child or a child who has formed only a casual or diluted attachment with an adult is in serious danger. Rather than making the child stronger, this can lead to emotional disturbances and may decrease the child's ability to form close or lasting relationships with other people throughout adult life.

There are situations where a child's biological parent is functionally replaced by another adult, who becomes a psychological parent to the child. This rarely occurs in day care centers and day care homes, of course, but it occurs regularly in adoption and can sometimes happen in foster homes or with nannies. When this happens, the very young child comes to trust and depend on the nonbiological parent just as he or she would the natural parent, and forms a close primary attachment with that person. If this happens, it is not substitute care. That term is not appropriate here. Emotionally, it is the real thing.

When a young child is living with the biological parents but is cared for primarily by a live-in nanny, au pair, or daytime baby-sitter, the child may form a primary attachment to one of the parents or to the hired caretaker. This depends on a number of factors, including the amount of time the parents spend with the child, the age of the child when the arrangement is begun, and the ability and willingness of the child care provider to dependably meet the child's daily needs. In some cases a young child may have no attachment or only a weak attachment to the biological parent.

A sitter with two children of her own told the following story of a fourteen-month-old child who had been in her care since she was two weeks old. On weekends the child was cared for by a different sitter while her parents jogged and played tennis. "When her mother comes for her at six and picks her up, she reaches her little arms out to me, calling, 'Mama, mama,' as she's being carried out the door. Calling, 'Mama, mama,' to *me*. It breaks my heart."

Because young children's emotional needs are very strong, they will, over time, form a primary attachment to any person who interacts with them on a very constant and reliable basis, even if that person is callous or emotionally disturbed. Victims of parental child abuse are usually very attached to that parent. Conversely, young children do not form a strong attachment to a person they see little of, no matter how kindly the person is or how superlative the quality of the time spent together. As a grandfather flying in for a one-year birthday celebration discovers, to his dismay, blood ties alone mean nothing to the baby. The birthday boy or girl may treat him like a stranger.

The day care decision can have an impact on either the formation of an attachment or the strength of that attachment, depending on the age of the child, the type of day care, and the family situation. Once the bonding process is understood, and parents understand the needs of very young children, they will discover that they are approaching the day care decision from a very different perspective; planning will be based on a careful strategy to meet those needs.

Types of Substitute Care

If a child's basic need for bonding is being met, a preschool or nursery school experience can be a wonderful thing for three- to five-year-old children. Between two and a half and three, children become ready to play cooperatively with other children, and a group play experience with peers becomes important for the child's social development. At this age children learn to share, and dramatic play becomes more elaborate. Preschoolers can spend two or three hours away from their parents without anxiety, and almost always enjoy the chance to make new friends, play with different toys, and make wonderful, creative messes with finger paints, clay, and other delightful substances many mothers are not overly fond of.

Nursery schools are usually morning programs, which a child typically attends two, three, or five mornings a week. The better ones are staffed by teachers trained in early childhood education. Good nursery schools are for children. Their entire purpose is to create a setting in which three- to five-year-old children will have an enjoyable learning experience. Some nursery schools stress social aspects, while others emphasize skills intended to give the children a head start in language arts and math, but all are child-oriented.

Although the better day care centers also have toys and offer some craft projects, they are basically parent-oriented. Their function is to provide a safe place for children to stay while their parents are at work. *Day care center* usually refers to a center that cares for children from potty training until kindergarten. There is often only one adult for each ten or even fifteen children.

Centers that care for babies under three are often called infant centers, but may be called day care centers too. There are also mixed-age day care centers, which care for children from infancy until kindergarten full time, and have before- and after-school care for children from kindergarten through third grade.

Day care centers are usually open ten to twelve hours a day, and serve two or three meals a day. Usually the staff of a day care center is not trained in early childhood education. It is not considered necessary, since the primary function of a day care center is not to teach children but simply to care for them.

Although the quality of both nursery schools and day care centers varies considerably, the number of hours a child spends away from parents is a very important consideration. The best-quality group care is no substitute for the bonding process with caring parents.

If group care must be considered, arrangements should be chosen very carefully. While group care in day care homes and centers cannot satisfactorily fill a child's basic emotional needs, callousness and insensitivity certainly are to be avoided; a full-time day care infant, toddler, or preschooler, who is already feeling lonely, abandoned, or rejected, needs support and understanding. Sometimes the attitude can be quite cold. A mother entering an infant center saw two child care workers having coffee. Her baby was crying in his crib. She overheard the newly hired child care worker ask, "Should I pick him up?" and the one who had been there for some time reply complacently, "Oh, never mind that one, he's just spoiled."

If more lengthy care than preschool must be considered, it is important to realize there are differences in the quality of care: for example, between commercially run and nonprofit centers.

Help Wanted

Freelance agency handling account for provider of day care is developing a marketing campaign, aimed at children 3–6, with thrust a character named Cuddlypoo. Young, small, cuddly, fun, bear-like creature, featured eventually in animated commercials, premium items, logos, etc. Job is designing the Cuddlypoo.

In 1958 the majority of children whose mothers worked full time were cared for at home. The 1970s saw a shift to group care. Today, 15 percent of children under six in the United States are cared for in full-time day care centers. Sixty percent of these are commercial day care centers, which have corporate profits as their first priority. They are typically owned by businessmen, not educators, and staffed by women who get little more than minimum wage. The child:adult ratio is usually the maximum allowed by law. The services of these centers are packaged and sold like any commercial product; parents are not supposed to look deeper than the image of the Cuddlypoo.

The majority of nonprofit day care centers are church-run, but there are many private nonprofit centers as well. Some offer a sliding fee scale based on parents' income. Nonprofit centers are eligible for various grants and government funds that profit-making centers cannot apply for, so in general they have slightly better child:adult ratios and are a little better equipped. The better infant centers have one adult who is assigned to no more than four babies, but if babies are at the center ten or twelve hours a day, there will still be at least one change of shift. Then there are vacations and days "their" person is out sick. In addition, because in the United States child care is low-status work, there is a problem of job turnover as workers "burn out" and look for other employment.

One disadvantage of day care centers, profit and non-profit alike, is that, like any institution, they involve a certain amount of regimentation. A center can rarely accommodate toddlers who need a longer, shorter, or earlier nap than their peers. A child's individual rhythms must be subjugated to the group's schedule. In a poorly run center this lack of flexibility can be very hard on children. One of the authors was in a county-run center and heard a preschooler wailing in the bathroom. As she approached to see what the problem was she heard the staff person standing over the child saying, "This is peeing time, so you are going to pee."

Fifty-six percent of children in full-time day care are cared for in a home other than their own. Many of these children are in licensed and unlicensed day care homes, where one woman cares for a number of children in her own house. Day care homes are as variable as the day care providers. Some offer crafts and activities, while in others children sit in front of a TV set eating saltines and drinking Kool-Aid.

The worst cases of abuse usually occur in homes rather than centers, because day care mothers, unlike day care workers, usually have no peer surveillance. Unlike Denmark, where a social worker does an unscheduled inspection twice a month, there is virtually no checking up on day care homes here in the U.S. Periodically stories hit the newspapers—children injected with tranquilizers and locked in closets, children beaten and deprived of food and water. County licensing agencies usually rely on complaints to detect a problem, but parents are often hesitant to file a complaint and want to believe Tommy did get that bruise from a fall.

About one quarter of children whose parents work full time are cared for in their home by a nanny, housekeeper, au pair, or baby-sitter. This kind of child care is expensive for the parent, since anyone doing child care over twenty hours a week must be paid minimum wage. Even when the salary is good, parents cannot make this low-status job really attractive. Usually child care positions are stopgaps for students or newly arrived immigrants who will go on to other fields, or they are taken by women who feel they have no other job skills, although this may slowly begin to change with the recent advent of schools to train professional nannies.

This one-to-one kind of arrangement is the only form of day care that has the potential to actually supplement or even replace the child's bonding with the parents. If a caretaker stays with a child for a period of years, the child may form a secondary attachment to this person, just as he or she might to a grandmother, even if the primary attachment is to the mother. This may meet some of the child's emotional needs. However, from the caretaker's side, the nanny, au pair, or baby-sitter may not want to form a close relationship to the child knowing that relationship may soon end. The au pair knows she will return home in one year, and the sitter may have future job plans. A caretaker is in an emotionally vulnerable position if she allows herself to grow to feel that her charge is really like a son or daughter. The child in her care is *not* her own child, and a dispute with the child's parents over an issue such as discipline could end with a dismissal that would be emotionally traumatic for the caretaker as well as the child.

Many mothers give a double message to nanny: I want you to love the baby—but not *too* much. They find it hard to miss their babies' "firsts" and to know that their baby is spending most waking hours with a nanny. They are often unsure of their decision to work, and feel so fragile that when Baby cries as Nanny leaves at 6:00 P.M. they fall apart. One response to this jealousy is to break the attachment, to get a new nanny. This, of course, is the worst thing for the baby. The baby needs to feel loved, and it is only natural for a nanny to want the baby to love her in return. Love cannot be a one-way street. Some mothers do not understand that if they do find "loving care" for their baby, that baby may grow to love the caretaker. As Dr. Berry Brazelton of Harvard Medical School pointed out in an interview with one of the authors, "Parents do grieve. They're no longer important to the child. Jealousy of the caretaker is inevitable, and they act it out in various ways." For in-the-home care to succeed, parents need to find an exceptional person *and* to have enough patience and self-understanding to develop a good working relationship with that person.

Day Care and Children with Special Needs

It is unfortunate that one event that frequently catapults young children into day care is a divorce. "If Mommy and Daddy could stop loving each other, then perhaps they could stop loving me." Children who have seen Mommy or Daddy walk out and not return often worry that they will be left stranded at day care, that their parents will not return for them.

These feelings of insecurity and abandonment are worst when a child senses a parent really does wish to be free of the burden of parenthood. "I loved being in high school. If I've got to be single again then I'd like to go back to those fun times," a young divorcée wished. "But it's different now, I've got them," she added, referring to her two preschool daughters.

Divorce is very hard on young children. They are faced with one parent's being away, and sometimes a move to a new home and new neighborhood as well. Having to adjust to Mommy's starting to work full time in addition can stress a young child to the breaking point.

There are other children besides children of divorce who are under stress that may cause them to become disruptive in a group care situation. These "problem children" need additional understanding and attention, yet the overburdened day care provider is not likely to be patient with a child who makes her job harder. The colicky infant, the child with a disfiguring birthmark, the baby with a physical ailment that causes crankiness, all need extra attention. Yet these children are in the worst position when it comes to inspiring affection in the group day care provider.

Severe family disturbances such as alcoholism, drug addiction, and child abuse put children at risk. The likely results of such a troubled family background are well known. However, day care is not an answer for these unfortunate children. Because the children's emotional needs are not being met in a critical stage of their development, taking them away eight or ten hours a day does not solve the problem. In most cases, family counseling, parent education, and specify therapy for drug or alcohol addiction or for child abuse would enable the parents to begin to relate to and care for the children and would benefit the entire family.

In those cases where this type of support fails, the children should be placed in a foster home or other situation where they can have an opportunity to form a close attachment with a substitute parent. The victims of violence or neglect badly need to form a close bond with a nurturing parent substitute, and full-time group day care does not provide this.

The Parents' Role

Good day care versus bad day care is not the primary issue. Full-time day care, good or bad, can and usually does interfere with the fundamental emotional development of young children and the formation of a close attachment to their parents. When parents consider substitute care arrangements, the age of the child and the potential effect on the bonding process with the parents should be a primary consideration. The amount of separation is very significant. A child can feel all degrees of attachment toward his or her parent, but only a very close attachment can satisfy the child's very intense need.

So parents really are in a position to try to create and maintain a truly close relationship with their child. In making the day care decision, parents themselves hold the key to their children's emotional well-being.

Chapter Two

The Day Care Debate

The scientific investigation of the nature of bonding and the emotional needs of children has become the focus of the day care debate. Rapid social change and increasing day care enrollment challenge our basic assumptions about child raising and have put tremendous pressure on child-development experts to give us answers to questions about the effects of separation from the parents, the effects of group day care, and the length of separation children at various ages can handle without an emotional deficit.

However, we should point out that although the changes in family life *have* been dramatic, they have frequently been distorted and exaggerated. Articles such as the one that appeared in *Women's World* (November 30, 1982) typically note that "nearly half of all married women with children under six are now in the labor force," implying that these children are in day care. In fact, about one fifth of children whose mothers work full time are cared for by the father or by the mother herself while she works; these situations can hardly be called day care. When mothers work part time, as *nearly half* of all married working mothers do, the figure is even higher and *two out of every five children* will be cared for by their father or mother. Once relatives other than the parents are included, a clearer picture emerges: half of all children whose mothers work full time are cared for by a family member or relative, and when a mother works part time only one child in three is cared for by someone other than a parent or relative.

Nevertheless, there has been a shift away from in-home care. In the last fifteen years the number of children enrolled in day care centers has more than quadrupled, and, as mentioned earlier, centers now account for the care of 15 percent of all children whose mothers work full time.

The findings of a survey by *Family Circle* magazine (February 20, 1979), which show that only one mother in ten would use a relative if she had a choice, indicate that the use of center-based care is likely to continue to grow. Although most Americans find repugnant the current Chinese system of placing eighteen-month-old babies in round-the-clock day care six days a week, center-based daytime care for infants and young children is an option many working American parents are now ready to consider.

These changes in the family have created the day care debate, particularly a debate about group and center-based care, and educators and child-development experts are anxious to answer parents' and the society's questions about day care's effects on children. Currently, psychologists and educators are deeply divided on this question. The opinions range from strong criticism and concern to an emphatic assertion that lengthy separation has no negative effects on children's development. This chapter looks at the controversy surrounding this issue and examines the frequently heard claim that studies have given full-time day care a clean bill of health.

Studying Attachment: Problems and Perils

The good news is that the number of investigations examining the effects of alternative care arrangements has increased substantially during the past eight years; the bad news is that when considered from a broader

> perspective on human development we know shockingly little about the
> impact of day care on children, on their parents, and on the society in
> which these children and parents live.
>
> Jay Belsky and Laurence Steinberg
"The Effects of Day Care: A Critical Review"
(*Child Development*, 1978, volume 49, 929–49)

While there is a general agreement among developmental psychologists and child psychiatrists that the first two or three years are particularly crucial to a child's emotional development and that a close, enduring relationship is the foundation of a child's emotional well-being, scientific investigations have not been able to make any definitive statement about the effects of various kinds of part-time and full-time day care on the emotional attachments between a child and the parents. Belsky and Steinberg's critical review of more than forty studies, which appeared in *Child Development*, confirmed suspicions in the scientific community that existing studies are seriously flawed or very narrow and therefore grossly inadequate. Currently there is no way to accurately measure whether a young child's emotional needs are being met in various day care arrangements, or to measure the long-term effects of lengthy separation on emotional development into adulthood. Studies have been unable to establish a minimum requirement for daily contact and interaction between parents and their children.

Some researchers and many advocates of full-time day care have claimed that studies prove that day care is harmless or even beneficial to children's emotional development, and this message has frequently been repeated in books and magazine articles. This is far from the truth. As Belsky and Steinberg note in their article, referring here to all aspects of a child's development, "To even say that the jury is still out on day care would be in our view both premature and naively optimistic. The fact of the matter is, quite frankly, that the majority of the evidence has yet to be presented, much less subpoenaed."

Parents often wonder about studies and are puzzled by conflicting claims. On the surface, it would seem that careful, well-designed studies should be able to resolve this issue. The authors do not recommend that parents ignore the ongoing research on day care, but we feel it is necessary that parents understand the limitations so that premature or inappropriate conclusions become easier to identify. A critical approach can reveal what is really worthwhile and relevant.

There are two main approaches to the study of day care's effect on the attachment between a child and the parent, and these can be used to examine a child's attachment to a parent or the parent's bond to the child. The first approach is the experimental study of behavior, often done in a laboratory setting. In the better studies, trained observers are often instructed to note certain behaviors without knowing the hypothesis of the experiment, or which subjects are really part of the experiment and which are in a control group. If the results are really meaningful, it should be possible for other researchers to replicate the experiment with the same results. The second approach is psychoanalytic, whereby a trained investigator examines a child's emotional adjustment by listening to reports of dreams, having the child make up and act out stories, interpreting drawings, and so forth. The main failing in this approach as an exclusive tool to gain knowledge is that different investigators may interpret a child's stories or fantasies differently, and it may be difficult to establish a consensus. Thus, these findings are sometimes termed "soft data."

But the experimental studies that are supposed to yield objective, "hard" data have produced data that does not support anything but the narrowest conclusions. One type of study examines day care children's interaction with their mothers and their day care workers in a laboratory setting. Dale Farran and Craig Ramey's 1977 study (*Child Development*, 1977, volume 48, 1112–16) involved giving a day care child a cookie in a tightly sealed transparent container in the presence of both the mother and the day care provider. They found that of the children who requested help, all turned to their mother. This type of study raises more questions than it answers. First, it is unclear whether the child's preference for the mother in this situation is related to feelings of attachment. The child may be responding to learned expectations from previous situations.

But even if we assume that this preferential behavior does indicate that the child is more attached to the mother than to the day care provider, these crude indicators do not mean that the relationship between the mother and child has not been affected by the use of substitute care. As we said in Chapter 1, there are degrees of closeness; we cannot simply say a relationship exists or does not exist. The fact that day care children choose their mother over the day care provider may mean that the mother-child relationship is stronger than the day care provider–child relationship, *but it does not show that the relationship is as close as it would have been if the children had been reared at home.*

Another type of experiment has been used to try to determine the degree of attachment between mother and child. These situations are variations of Mary Ainsworth and Barbara Wittig's 1969 "strange situation" experiment (in B.M. Foss [editor], *Determinants of Infant Behavior*, vol. 4, London: Methuen, 1969). A mother brings her child into a room with a stranger, and a few minutes later, with no warning or explanation, leaves the room. Some researchers believe that by observing the child's responses to the mother's leaving and to her return, and the child's interaction or lack of interaction with the stranger, the quality of the mother-child relationship can be determined.

Results of these experiments have not been consistent. J. Conrad Schwarz, David Corsini, and Debbie Moskowitz (*Child Development*, 1977, vol. 48, 1271–76) found that home-reared children showed more distress upon separation from their mother. Moncrieff Cochran (1977) and Henry Ricciuti (1974) found that day care children showed greater distress. Another study by Fern Portnoy and Carolyn Simmons (*Child Development*, 1978, vol. 49, 239–42) failed to discover any day care/home difference. Even if the results of these experiments had not been so contradictory, the meaning remains unclear. Shall we say if home-reared children cry more that they are more attached? Or shall we say if home-reared children cry less it is because they are more secure, and the day care children are showing their insecurity by crying when separated from their mothers? Or should we conclude that day care children are simply more accustomed to being left, and that it is a matter of habit when they don't cry and has nothing to do with their degree of attachment? Many researchers question whether separation-anxiety experiments are any measure of the quality of a mother-child relationship. The variable results suggest that they may be right.

Interestingly, there is one area not directly related to the issue of attachment in which studies have found a reasonably consistent and predictable difference between home-reared and day care children, and that is in the children's social behavior toward adults. While day care children tend to be more peer-oriented, there is also a marked difference in their interaction with adults. Day care children, particularly from all-day group settings, tend to be more physically and verbally aggressive, less cooperative, and have a lower tolerance for frustration. This "aggressiveness" finding has stimulated a rather heated debate, with conclusions ranging from a direct condemnation of group day care to the overly optimistic conclusion that ͏ children are merely more independent and mature.

Belsky and Steinberg in their review suggest that day care chi͏ ͏en are precociously assimilating the "characteristically stressed American values of aggressiveness, impulsivity, and egocentricism," and that is behind the differences uncovered in these studies. However, even if that is the explanation, it is hardly a desirable trend, and they recommend that group care programs be reevaluated in an attempt to counteract this phenomenon. Whether this aggressiveness reflects a change in the intensity or quality of attachment of day care children to their parents is an open question.

Because the results of the experimental approach to the study of day care's impact on attachment have been inconclusive, the psychoanalytic investigation of human relationships still provides the most useful basis for understanding attachment and the effect of substitute care. Although there is a problem of bias and subjectivity of individual investigators, this approach has provided a wealth of insights into the basic nature of human attachments. As Freud discovered, children, like adults, possess an unconscious mind, and events in early childhood may have a profound effect on an adult, even though that adult may be completely unaware of this and may not consciously recall the experience. Most of the experiences of early childhood, including very psychologically painful ones, are not normally remembered by an adult, but they are stored in the unconscious. Early experiences representing unmet emotional needs are etched in the child's unconscious mind.

Well-known British psychoanalyst John Bowlby combined the disciplines of psychoanalysis, ethology, feedback theory, and studies of cognitive development in his recently completed trilogy *Attachment and Loss* (Basic Books, 1980) to shed light on the nature of human attachment. While Bowlby is reluctant to "lay down the law" about the precise acceptable limits of separation in the first years, he concludes that a child who does not have a stable attachment to a parent or parent substitute will have emotional difficulties. As discussed in Chapter 1, many other psychoanalysts have come to the same conclusion.

Unfortunately, neither Bowlby nor other investigators have done systematic long-term and retrospective psychoanalytic studies of the effects on attachment of various types of day care, and it will take many years of the "day care experiment" before this data is available.

It is much easier to answer questions about what is optimal to ensure a close attachment than it is to predict the exact effects of a diluted bond. At present there is insufficient information to make precise statements about the specific effects of a certain length of separation at a particular stage of development.

Because of the substantial limitations on research, parents must be very wary of false claims that the scientific community has given day care a clean bill of health. Most of us would not want the Food and Drug Administration to adopt a policy that new drugs could be introduced on an "innocent until proven guilty" basis. While this may be a good principle for our judicial system, it would be disastrous for the introduction of new medications into our society. Without the safeguards of extensive trials in animals and controlled clinical studies in humans prior to marketing, a new medication could have harmful effects before anyone could prove beyond a doubt that it was responsible for such effects. Even with the existing safeguards, such tragedies have occurred. But, of course, there has been no equivalent certification of day care prior to its adoption. Day care as it exists is the experiment; and how soon we will be able to accurately measure its effects on emotional development is unknown.

Availability of Information

Unfortunately, the information that does exist about the potentially harmful effects of full-time day care has frequently been distorted or suppressed, because day care has become a political issue. The choices of what aspects of day care are studied, how the studies are designed, and how the data is interpreted are subject to tremendous pressure from political and ideological forces in the women's movement as well as pressure from a growing day care industry. In addition, very important information from observations by day care providers and parents themselves has not been voiced in a climate that is often hostile to open questioning about the advisability of early separation of infants and toddlers from their parents.

After telling the authors of some serious problems she saw with full-time day care for young children, a professor of early childhood education at a major university in California added, "But all this is off the record. Politically I can't afford to be against day care." She was concerned about jeopardizing her position and support for her research.

Research in an unpopular area can be thwarted in a number of ways. Delayed publication, funding cuts, peer pressure, and actual threats are all real possibilities in the life of a researcher or academician who publishes or experiments in a politically sensitive area.

So the ivory tower of academia and scientific research is reliably neutral and unbiased only so long as it deals with relatively neutral subjects. While many researchers do try to remain objective and unbiased when working in an unpopular area, the absence of hard scientific proof in the day care debate has led many experts to hide their suspicions or reservations about day care and adopt an officially neutral or even pro–day care position, thereby avoiding the unpleasantness of intense criticism and political pressure. We feel that many of these same professors who are taking a neutral position on the day care issue would openly express their reservations and concerns in a climate where such an attitude was welcome, or at least acceptable.

The dramatic reversals of position of some of the well-known researchers and psychologists on the day care issue in recent years raises questions about trends and pressures. In December 1970 Harvard psychologist Jerome Kagan was the coauthor of "Day Care Can Be Dangerous" (*Psychology Today*), yet today he is a staunch supporter of full-time day care. Other psychologists have made similar changes in their position, in spite of the fact that there has been no dramatic breakthrough in our knowledge about day care's effect on bonding. Particularly disturbing is the tendency of some of these authorities to talk about the needs of parents rather than of children when challenged on this point.

To make matters worse, many researchers and academicians are parents and are not above the social and economic pressures on family life in contemporary society. When the authors interviewed a professor of early childhood education at a large Eastern college and asked what she knew about the effects of day care on children, her first response was a defensive "My son was in day care from the time he was one and a half, and he turned out fine." This did not seem like an appropriate professional response to the question. Having put her own child in day care, she apparently found it extremely difficult to maintain objectivity about the issue. And one wonders, from the sudden change of tone and defensiveness when the question was asked, whether this professor and mother may herself harbor some reservations about her decision.

Since many researchers who are currently studying day care are parents who put their own children in day care, this may be a significant limitation on the books and articles these researchers have published. When researchers know a study showing that day care has harmful effects would have disastrous political effects within the university, and additionally know that such a finding would mean that they had personally made a serious mistake in raising their own children, the direction of their research and the types of studies they design may be affected. And, of course, an unbiased interpretation of the results may be very difficult.

Although young children are not very articulate, they often do express their unhappiness about being in day care, in a variety of ways. This is an important kind of information, which is usually suppressed or downplayed by day care providers. When a day care worker from Pennsylvania started work at a center, she noticed that three-and-a-half-year-old Eric would frequently walk off into a corner of the room crying and asking for his mommy. She asked the director if it was the policy to tell parents if a child complained about being at the center. The director replied, "Sometimes it's hard for children to adjust. But we don't tell the parents about it. It makes them feel guilty."

If, in spite of this censorship, parents become aware of the fact that their children are unhappy in day care, they usually assume that it is the fault of the particular sitter, the day care home, or the day care center. Day care providers know this all too well, and they naturally want to avoid friction, criticism, confrontations, and possible bad will and loss of business. Not relaying these youngsters' distress calls is the easiest path. Unwittingly, parents may contribute to this vicious circle by assuming that any complaints that they hear mean that the current day care arrangement is not satisfactory and must be replaced by a better day care arrangement. One survey found that three out of five mothers had changed day care arrangements within a two-year period, more than half of these because they were dissatisfied. But very often the child is complaining about the lengthy daily separation from the parent, not about the condition of the toys or the careless attitude of one of the day care workers. The net result of all this is that the message that day care itself is causing a problem rarely gets through.

Even when there is no stated policy about relaying complaints to parents, most day care workers are reluctant to do so. They are afraid that they will be personally blamed for the child's unhappiness: "Can't you keep him happy? It's your job, isn't it?" Indeed, the authors felt this expectation when they were day care providers; there was a strong tendency to measure the success or failure of a day care program by the "adjustment" of the children. It took some time for us to realize that the children often were unhappy and missed their parents *despite* our doing a good job of meeting their individual needs and keeping them actively involved in projects and activities throughout the long day. There is a natural tendency for conscientious day care workers to define their job as keeping the children happy. They know that parents expect this. A day care worker who does express concerns to a parent may be seen as a traitor by the other workers. The other workers often feel that the concerned worker is in effect telling the parent that *they* are not doing a good job. So there is strong peer pressure not to speak out or question the underlying assumption that "the kids are okay."

In the day care situation children are usually discouraged in a variety of ways from expressing anything negative about being there. These can range from children's perceptions of the expectations of the day care providers to more direct systems of rewards and punishments. Complainers are often ostracized. "Look at Tommy. He's a big boy. He doesn't cry for his mommy all the time."

Day care children who are unhappy and seek more individual attention are in a bind. They can sense that constantly asking for their parents is not what the day care provider wants to hear, and if they keep it up they are likely to get less attention, not more. And if they express their feelings to their parents, they may find that a tired working parent is not overjoyed at the prospect of trying to find another suitable and affordable day care arrangement. Just like adults, children can begin to feel that they have no choice, and they will become reconciled to their fate. They may stop expressing their feelings to the day care workers and their parents, but these feelings have not evaporated, and a child may suddenly become more aggressive or demanding. Children can act out their feelings in many ways.

It is surprising how very young children may hide their feelings or hold them inside. Janet Latoures, a social worker who is on a leave of absence to raise her child, left her twenty-six-month-old daughter with a friend for a couple of hours. "My friend said Mireille didn't cry. She just grew very quiet. It was only when my friend asked, 'Do you miss your mommy?' that her eyes filled up and her chin began to quiver. In a day care center they probably would have told me, 'She did just fine, she didn't cry.'" Just as two-year-olds can hide their feelings, so can day care children who are three, four, and five. At the authors' day care center it was not uncommon for four- and five-year-old children who had never openly complained about being in day care to dictate entries in their private journals complaining about the long hours of separation and how they wished their mother didn't work.

Concurrent with the suppression of information in various kinds of day care arrangements and the bias in academia, there have been many instances of extreme bias in the mass media. Despite numerous articles in the medical journals describing significant health risks associated with group care for very young children, this issue has, up to the present time, received virtually no coverage in the mass media. (These health problems will be discussed in Chapter 5.) And women's and family magazines have almost exclusively played it safe, focusing on the "good day care versus bad day care" issue, or the needs of parents, and avoiding any criticism of full-time day care per se. Popular topics are how to choose a day care center and how to cope with being a "superwoman." A 1978 *Family Circle* magazine article by Jane Whitbread gave several examples of anguished day care children asking Mommy not to go to work, and then concluded that the children are fine and it was pointless and self-defeating for parents to worry that there might be something wrong. Bring home a special treat in the evening, it advised, and the child will forget all about his or her unhappy day. By all means, avoid feeling overly guilty.

This guilt issue keeps coming up again and again. One magazine writer, who is working part time and sharing child-raising responsibilities, submitted an article critical of day care to a national women's magazine, and received a rather heated rejection: "We can't afford to make our readers feel guilty," concluded the editor. The authors concur, but from a very different point of view. It is important that the day care problem be recognized and appropriate actions be taken to correct the situation. Then there will be no guilt or concern, because there will be no problem. Concern can be a positive force that can become the basis for change.

Marshall McLuhan was right when he said that the medium is the message; and this idea can be extended to information's being profoundly affected by the weight or emphasis it receives in mass-media coverage. Even when there isn't censorship of day care criticism, the extent of coverage can determine the message that is conveyed. No wonder equal time has become a major issue in a mass-media society. Imagine reading the daily paper. On the second page there is a small article: "Border Fighting Erupts Between China and Russia." Just by emphasis, which is the editor's decision, we tend to downplay the small article in our minds. The facts may not warrant this; an article containing the same information but with a front-page headline would be quite alarming. Like it or not, we all are dependent on the selective process of the mass media; it is very difficult to remain unaffected by the emphasis given to a particular story or set of facts.

The authors have followed the media, and so far the coverage of day care has been overwhelmingly oriented toward the needs of working parents, working women, women's organizations, and changes in the family. There has been little coverage of *children's* needs or exploration of the potential harmful effects of full-time separation on young children.

Part of this suppression of opposing viewpoints and distortion of research in women's and family magazines is because many editors are women who have, or have had, their own children in day care. Like researchers, women editors who have made the decision to put their children in day care may be on the defensive. The suggestion that day care may be harmful is very threatening, and they have difficulty considering such an idea with an open mind. When personal considerations are compounded by marketing pressures there is little chance an article raising questions about the advisability of day care will be published in these magazines.

In the midst of the ongoing day care controversy, parents faced with the day care decision and those who have already placed their children in day care need to beware of self-serving research, premature conclusions, and a heavy bias in the media. We are living in a time of rapid change. A short time ago, the women's movement put the image of a full-time working mother up on a pedestal. Millions of women were working double-duty and wondering why they weren't feeling "liberated." Now, as it has become clear that working full time and trying to raise a family is a very stressful situation for a woman, the superwoman ideal is being questioned.

The day care experiment is also beginning to be questioned. Parents are beginning to question a system in which their young children spend most of their waking hours away from the family and to question the assumption that day care is the Way of the Future. Parent should not have to choose between financial security and caring for their children. Parents are beginning to speak out, and that is a healthy thing.

Chapter Three

Inside Day Care: A Child's-Eye View

Inside Day Care

The authors' personal experiences as day care workers and directors revealed a facet of full-time day care, reflected in the following material, that was not being covered in the constant flow of books and magazine articles on the subject. We were unprepared for the children's protestations, anger, and sadness, and were dismayed at the prospect of a negative experience for some of the children at our school. How the *children* were feeling about day care became a major concern of ours; something that was given little attention at that time by writers and educators.

One of the authors, Wendy Dreskin, kept a journal of events she observed while directing and teaching at the preschool and later at the preschool–day care center. The following are excerpts from a record of those years, including material from the children's dictated journals and letters, and parents' comments, that expressed the children's feelings about full-time day care. All the material is verbatim, though the names have been changed.

BARRY AND BILLY

Billy, my usually good little Billy, is crying. And the minute he starts, his brother Barry starts. The moment he can, Billy is out the door, running for the parking lot. I have to drag him back. He refuses to be held. He screams louder if I come near.

"Shall I spank him?" his dad asks me.

Here is a child frightened to the core, craving reassurance, needing to know that he is loved and that he is not being abandoned. He will certainly not get a message of comfort from a spanking. Besides, I have never known spankings to be a particularly reliable way to get children to *stop* crying.

"No, I wouldn't advise it," I say quietly. "Maybe you could try talking to him."

I know that Billy and Barry's father is anxious to leave for work, but I hate to see him leave while the boys are still so upset. I hope that Billy will respond to some quiet talking, to reminders that Mommy and Daddy love him and will be back to get him as soon as they finish work.

His dad tries reasoning. But it is too emotional an issue for reason to prevail. Billy keeps crying.

"Some babies go to day care at six weeks." His dad raises his voice in frustration. "Billy had two and a half years at home with his mother, and instead of gratitude I get this." He points to Billy, now face down on the hallway floor, watering it with his tears.

How can I tell him that two and a half years is not long enough? And how can I explain those tears are healthy?

I try to explain that the crying is healthy, healthier than the passiveness of the child zombies who let themselves be led off by any adult because all adults are interchangeable and faceless in the absence of love. Crying shows caring. I would be more worried about Billy if he didn't cry.

Billy cries for two hours. He spurns all attempts to comfort him. He doesn't want his older brother, his friends, or any of his teachers. He wants his Mommy or his Daddy. Period.

I think back to the months when Billy and Barry came as preschoolers, before their mother got a job. I accepted Billy even though he was only two years and eight months instead of the usual two years and nine months. Barry was four, and I'd found that bending the age rules usually worked out as long as there was an older sibling there for comfort.

It only took a few weeks for me to realize that it was Barry who relied on Billy. Billy is a solid little boy, physically and emotionally. Barry is thinner, and has more ups and downs. I don't think he has a level spot. In his ups he is a teacher's delight. He is bright and enthusiastic. I can almost see the light bulb light up in his head when he flashes on something I've said. In circle time he doesn't just raise his hand. His whole body shoots up like a spring, waving to be called on.

Barry sets very high standards for himself, and this is what usually causes the downs. Yesterday he tried to draw a picture of his mother with felt pens. It didn't come out the way he wanted. He said it didn't look like her, and tore it up and tried again. And again. And again. Each time he got more frustrated and tearful. By then a da Vinci wouldn't have satisfied him. He lay on the floor and wailed.

Billy, on the other hand, almost never cried as a preschooler. If he fell in the playground he would come over to sit in a lap, cry for a minute, and then turn to say with his usual smile, "All better!" Then he'd slide off the teacher's lap to return to the thick of things. He's always played with the four-year-old boys.

Billy and Barry's parents arranged a split shift so the boys would only have to spend six hours a day in the center. Their mother leaves for work early, and their father gets them up and dressed, makes them breakfast, and drives them to the center. Then their mother picks them up at 3:00 P.M. But for these children, even a six-hour day is too long. Having known them as preschoolers, I can see the strain the long day is putting on them.

TIMOTHY

One teacher opens the center at 7:30 A.M. By 9:00 A.M., when all the children have arrived for the day, there are sixteen children and two teachers. We also have a college work-study student. Some semesters student teachers from the college preschool-education program, or high-school students who are participating in a work-experience program, also come to learn and practice teaching at the center.

At noon some of the preschoolers go home, and some kindergarten children arrive for after-school care. Grade-school children arrive between 2:00 P.M. and 3:00 P.M. At 3:00 P.M. a new staff person arrives to relieve the teacher who opened up in the morning, and that person stays until the center closes at 6:00 P.M.

Timothy's mother has a three-year-old, a two-year-old, and a one-year-old. Even though she doesn't work, she has them in three different day care centers.

Timothy is three. He can hardly talk at all. The other children at school call him a baby. He usually plays in the block area, where we keep the building toys — hardwood blocks, colored blocks, Lincoln Logs, and Tinker Toys. There are small wooden people and animals to live in the worlds the children construct, and trucks, cars, fire engines, and trains to provide transportation.

"Choo-choo." Timothy points to a wooden train. He doesn't know some words an eighteen-month-old usually knows.

Although Timothy is an extreme, I notice that the day care children consistently have smaller vocabularies than the preschoolers. Children pick up new words in the process of making the daily rounds with their mothers. A curious "What's that?" at the shoe-repair shop, the gas station, or the produce section of the supermarket yields new vocabulary. Although we take the group on field trips to try to enrich their experience, the day care children do not catch up.

I think another factor besides wider experience is that by spending afternoons at home the preschoolers spend more time in conversation with adults. Even with a child:adult ratio of 5:1 or better, the day care children do not get to talk to adults as much as preschoolers do.

BARRY AND BILLY: TRYING A DIVERSION

Over the last two weeks Billy and Barry's crying has gradually been decreasing. Though they have by no means become resigned to their new schedule, they are at least approachable. We decided to try a new strategy today. At 9:00 A.M., when all the children sit down for music circle, Martha will intercept Barry and Billy when their dad drops them off and take them for a surprise walk to the pet store across the street.

It looks as if the plan will work. Martha is in the hallway when Barry and Billy's dad brings them, and I see their faces light up at her suggestion that they go to the pet store and see the puppies and kittens, just the three of them. They say good-bye to their dad with no tears, and off they go.

I am glad it went so smoothly. I can see their father looking more cheerful than he has for days as he heads for the office. I am about to start music time. But ... uh-oh! Allison has noticed Martha and Barry and Billy out one of the windows.

"Where is Martha taking Barry and Bill?"

I try not to lie to children unless it is absolutely necessary, so I explain. "Barry and Bill have been very unhappy lately when it's time to say good-bye to their daddy. We thought it might help them to feel better if they could go for a walk to the pet store with Martha."

Allison catches on immediately. "I miss my mommy too," she says with a pitiful pout.

"Me too."

"Me too."

I am just wondering what I've started when Susan pops up, "Well, I don't miss *my* mommy!"

"Me neither."

"Me neither."

"Me neither!"

I take a relieved breath. The snowball reaction is rolling the right way now. We can start music time.

In our culture songs are used for many purposes—to convey a folk or religious heritage ("Sweet Betsy from Pike," Christmas carols), to teach numbers or letters ("ABC," "Ten Little Indians"), to teach parts of the body ("Head and Shoulders, Knees and Toes"), and to teach foreign language ("Frère Jacques"). We enjoy all those songs at other times of the day, but this is a time for learning about music.

We distinguish between recreational music and a program that develops real musical skills. Drawing on the methods of the German composer Carl Orff, we have developed a music-education program. Children learn to distinguish between a rhythmic pattern and a beat when we do chants, to hear and move with the phrases of the music when we do song games, and to compose simple melodies.

It is a pleasure to see how the children progress when they have morning energy to put into learning music. In the elementary grades classroom music is often relegated to the afternoon times "when the children are too antsy to do anything else."

BUTCH

Noon, when the preschoolers get picked up, is always a hard time. Any day care children who are prone to miss their parents suddenly remember that it will be another five or six hours until they are picked up.

Butch has tears in his eyes. "I miss my mommy."

"Would you like to write her a letter, Butch?"

He brightens up a little, and goes to the art shelf to get a paper and felt pen.

He dictates: "I wish you didn't have to work, Mommy. I wish you could stay home and take care of me. I wish I could just come to school in the morning and then go home and have lunch with you. I like to go to school, but I don't like it all day because I want to play with you sometimes." He writes his name at the bottom, neatly folds the paper, and puts it in his cubby. He sees his lunch box there. He has calmed down enough to be interested in seeing what's in it, and soon after having investigated he has joined the others who are already eating lunch.

To an outsider the day care children at our center might seem unusually unhappy. This is because we always encourage them to talk about their feelings, positive or negative. In most day care situations there is a lot of pressure on children not to cry or complain. "Look at Johnny. He never cries for his mommy, he acts like a *big* boy. Why can't you be like him?"

Child care workers are usually more concerned with appearances than with the children's underlying feelings. When administrators see children crying, they usually blame the child care worker in charge. If tears and complaints continue, the day care worker may even risk being fired. This provides a very strong motivation for child care workers to discourage the expression of any negative feelings children may have about the day care center. Besides, from a practical standpoint, child care workers find it easier to care for children who are not always in tears. These pressures lead child care workers to use whatever strategies and manipulations are necessary to keep children from crying or complaining.

Although children's feelings don't change, their behavior is easily manipulated. When pressure tactics work (which is most of the time), child care workers can happily report to parents, "He's adjusted. He never cries anymore." Once children have realized that complaints in any form consistently bring censure or even punishment, even if they are directly questioned they will dutifully repeat that they like day care. A journalist who decided to go into a day care center and interview children to get their side of the story would have no trouble finding many children whose answers would make it seem they were happy and well adjusted.

Knowing that parents are likely to judge the quality of the center by "how happy" their child is makes honesty difficult. Almost all books and articles on choosing day care say that if a child cries after the first few days there is either something wrong with the day care situation or, if it is a good one, it is not the appropriate one for that particular child. Nowhere is it hinted that day care itself may be the problem, that children may cry or complain in the best of situations, because what they really want is to be with their parents.

When we first started day care I would have been in a real bind with a letter like Butch's. I would always have encouraged a child like that to express his feelings in a letter. But I would have been tempted to make sure the child "forgot" to take the letter home, feeling that the catharsis of writing it was sufficient. I would not have wanted to risk having the parent take the child out of the center unless there was another child on the waiting list. And even if there were, I would have worried that the mother would tell her friends the staff was incompetent because they were unable to keep the children happy.

Now I have no hesitation in letting Butch take the letter home. There is nothing we can do to make Butch truly happier, but there is something his mother could do. She works half time, and he comes eight hours a day, three days a week. It would be much better for him if he could come for fewer hours each day, even if it meant coming five days a week. Unfortunately, his mother does not want an arrangement that would increase her weekly commute time and expenses. I think she needs to hear Butch's message.

CONFERENCE WITH TIMOTHY'S MOTHER

I have asked Timothy's mother to come in for a conference. I am still concerned about his slow verbal development. I do not think his problem is physical, I would like to get her to admit there *is* a problem and to start thinking about it. I have decided to suggest a hearing test for a start, because I think the idea of having a child who is a little hard of hearing will be less threatening than the idea of a child that might have intellectual or emotional problems. I have checked into what county agencies will be able to help her. My hope is that when the test proves normal, I or the agency can suggest she look further for the source of Timothy's slow verbal development.

As I expected, she is very defensive. "His father didn't speak until he was four years old, and now he's a linguist and speaks eight languages." I appreciate the fact that she has bothered to come for a conference, but why does she come if she doesn't want to listen?

She obviously has no intention of taking Timothy for any sort of testing.

ALLISON

When she was three years old Allison used to come for preschool, but since her parents' divorce she is coming full time. She is a pretty child with soft, dark curls that always smell of shampoo.

Ginger is sitting in Martha's lap. Allison comes over and demands, "I want teacher's lap!" Ginger doesn't budge.

Suddenly Allison attacks, raking her nails across Ginger's face. She reminds me of a starving urchin fighting for a scrap of bread.

Martha stays calm. "You need to use words, Allison. You girls have a problem. Ginger wants my lap and Allison wants my lap. How can you girls solve this problem?"

They make suggestions, negotiate, and finally agree. When

the big hand gets on the 2 it will be Allison's turn in Martha's lap. At the appointed time Ginger relinquishes her place. Allison plops down. The raging wildcat has turned into a cuddly kitty. I can practically see her purr. We need about ten more laps around here.

It is interesting to see how the stress of day care affects different children. Some become withdrawn, while others become fighters, ready to do battle to get their share of attention. I always thought of Allison as such a sweet, affectionate, docile child. I would never have guessed she'd become one of the fighters. Her need must be very, very strong to drive her to take such drastic measures as hurting another child.

JASON

I'm worried about Jason. When he started preschool a year ago he was a joy to teach. At two years and nine months he knew all his colors, letters, and numbers. He was already very articulate, and enjoyed a wide range of activities from painting delicate watercolors to roaring around on a tricycle playing Batman.

Since his parents' divorce he has started coming five hours a day. He has lost interest in reading and most other activities. He insists nothing has changed at home. I can't get him to open up despite the good rapport we've always had.

But today it seemed to me he is finding a way to communicate. He went over to the illustration files, where we keep cut-out magazine pictures of people, animals, food, and so on. He chose pictures, arranged them in sequence, pasted them down on paper, and called me over, saying he wanted to dictate a story. I became excited when I realized the feelings he hadn't felt free to talk about were coming out in his story.

Ice Cream and Giving Kisses

Jason was coming to get some ice cream from the ice cream man. Linda did get some too. It was Robert who was giving it to them.

Linda was slopping her ice cream all over. She was sad because her dad told her not to get ice cream and she did anyway. She was afraid he'd be mad.

They went and picked some flowers for their mother and dad so they wouldn't be angry.

When they got home their mom and dad were fighting.

Mom said, "I don't like them eating ice cream 'cause it has too much sugar in it!"

Dad said, "It's okay if they do it!"

The children came home while they were fighting and they were sad. It made their mom and dad happy when the children gave them flowers. And then they kissed each other and the children were happy.

The arguments over what is "good" for him must seem endless to Jason. As the custody battle intensifies every unauthorized ice cream cone becomes a bullet. Both mother and father are determined to prove themselves as parents.

As the story shows, food is a major battleground. Jason was underweight even last year, and tension has not improved his appetite. The less he eats, the more his parents become concerned about what nutrition he is taking in. His mother is into health foods and doesn't eat much meat. His father feels that meat is the way for him to get the protein he needs.

"What was in your lunch box today?" has become a daily question, since the parent picking up is not the one who packed the lunch.

"Peanut butter and honey," grouses his father. "She gave you that Monday."

"No," replies Jason, the eternal diplomat, "Monday I had peanut butter and honey, but today I have honey and peanut butter!"

Divorce is always traumatic for young children, even in the rare instances when their parents separate amicably. Allison and Jason were in the best possible situation as far as there being a need for only a minimal amount of change. They could continue going to a familiar school with teachers they had known for over a year. The only difference was that they now had to stay longer.

The difficulties these two children are experiencing are certainly due to the divorce. But they are also due to their being in day care. When children feel insecure because of a divorce the last thing they need is to spend extra hours away from their source of security, their parents. Unfortunately, divorce often results in just that.

CHILDREN'S JOURNALS

Every child in the school has a journal. Some children dictate in them every day, while others feel inspired only once a week. There is no pressure or direction as to content. The children can say what they want on any subject. If children want their entries read aloud, we share them at story time.

Susan: "I love my mommy. I love my daddy. I love Jimmy, but sometimes I get mad at him when he breaks my toys. I have seven words in my word envelope."

Allison: "I love snack time. I love crackers with peanut butter. I love orange juice."

Billy: "In the morning I cry and want my mommy. Then I go to school."

Barry: "I like my mommy very much. She is so beautiful when she puts her dress on."

Jason: "Noodles are good, and they're legal, too!"

CARL

Six P.M. It is time to go home. Carl is getting his things out of his cubby. He leaves the little truck he brought this morning.

"Carl, don't you want to take your truck home?"

Sigh. "What's the use? I'm here more than I'm home anyway."

ROBERT

Four-and-a-half-year-old Robert is in the math/science area, playing with the set circles. He has made a set of red blocks and a set of triangles. He neatly overlapped the two set circles to show a set of red triangles. I suggest he draw a picture of what he has done in his math/science book. He eagerly goes to get felt pens and sets to work. He kneels on the floor, his silky red bangs flopping in his eyes. When he is done he calls me over to dictate. "I made a set of red things. I made a set of triangles. There are red triangles in the overlapping set."

I flip through his math/science book. He has nearly filled it up with his observations about what things in the room the magnet sticks to, how many days it took his corn to sprout, and how many "curlies" are in an alfilaria seed pod. He also has a graph of how many cars of each color are in the school parking lot, and one showing how many bicycles, cars, motorcycles, buses, and trucks passed the school in a fifteen-minute period. When his mother arrives at noon he will proudly show her his new entry in the math/science book. She doesn't lavish praise indiscriminately, but she always gives warm approval when he really has done a good job at some challenging task.

Parental expectations have a great effect on the children's achievements. Although a great variety of opportunities for learning exist at the center, I have noticed that one factor which affects how much children learn is how much their parents expect them to learn. The day care parents think of the center as a place for the children to play while Mom works, and convey this idea to their children. Some of them pay lip service to the idea of learning going on, and call the center "school," but they have no real expectations. They show no interest in looking at their children's journals, word envelopes, or math/science books. When day care children leave the center, these things are almost always left behind, unwanted, in the children's cubbies.

JASON "GETS LOST"

The fighting between Jason's parents is intensifying. The arguments over the division of money and possessions are bitter, and the ones over dividing Jason are worse. He is spending alternate nights with each parent. He can't keep his schedule straight, and often can't tell me who is supposed to pick him up or where he will sleep that night. Sometimes his parents can't keep it straight themselves, and they both show up at pickup time! Jason's most recent story was written with his friend Robert.

The Boy Who Was Lost

There was a boy who was lost. His name was Charlie.

He got lost in the trees. He was taking a walk and got lost.

He walked until he found a house. He was unhappy walking in the cold, and he was happy to find the house.

He decided to live in the house by himself. He took some money with him. He bought tents so he could camp in the snow. He felt like making snowballs and a snowman.

He went home and some of his friends came to visit — Fred and Charlie Brown and Robert and Jason and a girl named Sharon. The friends brought a camper with toys and food.

They ate salad with carrots and celery and radishes. And they had ice cream with nuts and whipped cream and a cherry. They all slept in the camper 'cause there were no beds in the house.

They liked it so much they stayed and never went back to their parents again. Their parents missed them, but they didn't miss their parents. They were happy.

Both Jason's parents must have had times they wished they could go about their lives without having to deal with him. He sensed that they resented him as the fruit of a love that no longer existed, and he, too, wished he could walk away from the situation and be on his own, with his own money, house, toys, food, and friends. The picture he chose of camping in the snow depicted the ultimate in getting away from it all — a base camp for an ascent of Mount Everest, with nothing but snowy peaks for miles around!

I think Jason felt very guilty about his wish. Robert wanted this to be a story about a boy who ran away, but Jason was adamant. Charlie did *not* run away — he *got lost*. Getting lost would be a way to escape everything without responsibility. If Charlie ran away the burden of his parents' unhappiness would be on him, and he would be less free to be happy in his independence. But in this story, although Charlie knows his parents are unhappy, he is off the hook, since he is lost and cannot return.

To further remove blame for himself, Jason did not use his own name this time, but made the story be about "Charlie." I am sure he was glad of this when his mother read the ending of the story and he saw tears in her eyes.

It might seem that with all the tension between his parents Jason would be better off at the center. But we don't feel this is the case. Despite his fantasy of getting away from his parents, now more than ever Jason needs to spend time with them and be reassured that both of them still love him.

FAILURE: ALLISON'S FATHER WILL NOT LISTEN

I know that Allison's father can afford to support her mother, at least for a year or two. I feel Allison would be on a much firmer footing if her mother could work half time until she is five. I discuss this with her mother, and then invite both parents to come for a conference.

I am pleased they are willing to sit down together to discuss their daughter. Not all divorced couples will. But Allison's father takes a firm stand. He can afford to support them, but he feels that if Allison's mother is not cooking and cleaning the house for him, there is no reason to support her. He sees making her take a full-time job as a sort of punishment. I try to point out that it is Allison who is getting punished. He understands. But if giving her what she needs means letting his ex-wife off easy, well, he's not going to do that, so Allison will just have to make the best of it.

PAUL

There is a little curtained-off area called the "Alone Place," cozy with a foam pad and pillows. Sometimes a child wants to get away from being with people for a while. The rule is that someone in there is not to be disturbed.

But, hearing crying, I look around the room to see who is not in sight. It's Paul again, a gentle, blond boy who comes six hours a day while his mother helps out at the family shoe store. He never makes a fuss when his mother leaves. He saves his soft tears for the privacy of the "Alone Place."

"May I come in?"
"Yes."
"Did someone hurt you, Paul?"
"No."
"Did someone say something that made you feel bad?"
"No."
"Can you tell me why you are crying?"
"I just feel sad inside."
"Would you like to be held?"

He crawls into my lap. I call to Bill and Martha that I'll be out of circulation for a while.

In a parent conference recently Paul's mother commented

that he used to be an outgoing, even belligerent child, and that he had suddenly changed when he was one and a half. We talked about other things, and then I happened to ask how long he had been in day care. "Since he was one and a half." Paul's mother is a well-meaning woman who obviously cares about her child, but she had never thought about the effects of day care. She had never connected the change in him with his entering day care.

Some studies suggest that full-time day care tends to produce aggressive children, but Paul has responded to the stress of day care by becoming very gentle and sensitive. Because of his own "sadness inside" he is very tuned in to what makes others unhappy, and would never hurt anyone else. What a different response from Allison's aggressiveness or Billy's wailing! Even at this age the children really are individuals.

CHILDREN'S JOURNALS

Billy: "I ate snack. I rode a trike. I played bad guys with Barry and Robert."

Susan: "I love my mommy. I love my daddy. I love Jimmy."

Paul: "My friend has a baby named Violet. I like Violet. Violet smiles at me."

Jason: "I had peanut butter and jelly for lunch."

Robert: "I went to my dad's office. He works up high on the seventh floor."

Allison: "I love my mommy so much I wish she didn't have to work."

A GROWING CONCERN

Bill and I are very troubled by all the problems of the day care children. We will have to discuss the problems of the program with the other board members.

Our Decision

The problem was not with our facility; the amount of toys and educational materials far exceeded the supplies of most centers. The problem was not our well-trained, credentialed staff; all staff members were qualified people who really liked and cared about young children. After two years of doing day care, it was obvious that there was a problem inherent in day care itself, a problem that hung like a dark storm over "good" and "bad" day care centers alike. The children were too young to be spending so much time away from their parents. They were like young birds being forced out of the nest and abandoned by their parents before they could fly, their wings undeveloped, unready to carry them out into the world.

So we decided to close the center. Once we realized day care was harmful to children we could not in good conscience continue to be day care providers, no matter how much people clamored about the need for day care in the community. We had been with the preschool for five years. Our preschool meant a lot to us. It was not an easy decision.

Chapter Four

Tuning In: Becoming More Sensitive to Your Child's Needs

Day Care: How We Got Here

The majority of parents do care about meeting their children's emotional needs. They are concerned about their children's development. Many children do tell their parents about their problems or complain. Yet most parents are not aware of the seriousness of the day care situation. Parents, and adults in general, find it difficult to separate children's real problems from everyday complaints and temporary emotional upsets. Parents sense that sometimes it is appropriate to be reassuring rather than concerned: "There, there, you'll be okay" or "Don't be frightened, it isn't real." But it is essential that serious problems be identified and dealt with; at times simple reassurance is not appropriate.

Discerning the effects of day care is not always easy. We frequently encountered misunderstandings in our interviews. A 32-year-old bank senior employment representative from Pennsylvania had her two-and-a-quarter-year-old daughter, Denise, in a full-day day care program three days a week. She felt uncomfortable with Denise's clinging and pleas to be held in the morning when she was dropped off at day care. "But," she added cheerfully, "I know she's really all right because she likes it so much she always cries when I come to pick her up at night!"

Lacking important information about the effects of day care on children's feelings of attachment, this mother had come to the wrong conclusion. Research in child development has shown that avoidance of the parent or primary attachment figure upon reunion and aggressive behavior are typical responses to the stress of separation for infants and toddlers (for example, Marie Blanchard and Mary Main, *Developmental Psychology*, 1979, vol. 15, no. 4, 445–46). Denise's tears when she was dropped off and when she was picked up *meant the same thing;* in both instances she was protesting the long separation from her mother.

Some parents try simple reassurances as an "acid test"; if the child stops crying or complaining, then it must not be important. However, there is no substitute for being knowledgeable about child development *and* having a parent's intuitive sense as well. Parents must know the child well enough to be able to tell what's trivial and momentary, and what is serious. Ruth Cohen, a full-time child raiser, says, "It's easy to get lost in the clichés and stereotypes of behavior, to act automatically. And the less time you give to it, the more this happens in a relationship." In this sense, full-time day care conspires against the child. How can parents be "tuned in" if they spend little time with their child? Of necessity, they depend on the day care provider's evaluation. One day care corporation even has the slogan "He stopped crying the minute you left." Of course, this is designed to encourage the parents to put any complaints they might hear in the "not serious" category. "No need to be concerned, she doesn't miss you at all."

In the last fifty years advances in the fields of psychoanalysis and child psychology have added to adults' awareness, and yet problems of understanding and respecting children's feelings have not evaporated. In spite of these limitations, the closeness in the traditional family provides a suitable environment for children. If the emotional needs are being met, then difficulties in defining those needs and deficits are less critical. On the other hand, with millions of children in some form of day care, a lack of awareness about the effects of day care on the part of parents and adults can have a disastrous effect on these children's emotional development.

In a fast-changing technological society, we are very used to experiments; we take this process for granted. The failures, the inventions that backfire, like DDT and thalidomide, are the price we pay for such rapid development. The emergence of the "day care experiment" makes our inability to separate the temporary and the trivial from basic emotional needs a critical issue for our children.

Most day care providers are not aware of the basic emotional needs of children. Many see their job simply as controlling children adequately so they do not hurt themselves or others, and making sure children eat their meals and take their naps. They are not really interested in or concerned with what makes children tick. A trained teacher might be better able to determine if a three-year-old's demeanor or a four-year-old's drawings and stories show a problem, but most day care providers do not have this training.

For the parent, getting to know the child as he or she really is, is essential in identifying unmet needs. No formula or generalization will do. "It says here in the manual that you should be happy, Johnny, so smile!"

A Stranger in Our Midst

"I like them [children] when they are beyond the amoeba stage," says a thirty-four-year-old stockbroker, discussing his two-and-a-half-year-old son. "When they are older, you can play baseball with them and go around and do things." In this fast-paced, high-pressure society, the early stages of infancy and childhood may seem like an inconvenience. "Hurry up," the parent may feel like saying. To paraphrase *My Fair Lady*'s Professor Higgins, who asks, "Why can't a woman be more like a man?", the parents sometimes wonder why children can't be more like adults. Is this slow early development really necessary?

The truth is that infants and toddlers are vastly different from ourselves; their conscious experiences are quite different from ours. The great irony is that we were all there once. We are like sleepers waking from a dream; we can't analyze it until we are awake. When we are old enough to begin asking what childhood is, we are no longer children, and in our conscious minds we remember little of our first few years.

Then we look to the experts to explain to us what these little people are thinking and feeling; most important, to tell us how our behavior and discipline will affect the child. It is as though parents have come in contact with a "primitive" tribe and are seeking the advice of a cultural anthropologist who specializes in that particular culture. With children and with the strange Pygmies from the forest, the questions would be the same: How can I communicate with them? How do they experience the world? How are they different from us? What do we have in common? Of course, the situations are not parallel in all respects, and parents are faced with additional difficulties. Parents must constantly refine and reevaluate their methods for encouraging the child to behave in a certain manner and to understand and accept the family values.

Mothers and fathers are often unsure if their approach to child raising is effective, and they may discuss their concerns with other parents, especially family members. If that resource is not available or satisfactory, then they often turn to books on child rearing, take classes in parenting, or even seek professional help.

A great deal is known about the physical and psychological development of infants and toddlers. Much has been learned through careful observation, studies, and experiments. But all adults, including the "cultural anthropologists"—the child-development experts —are looking at this "subculture" from the outside.

Much is not known and may never be known about the child's world. But just as the tourist to Bali who has read in his guidebook that he must not wear shorts in public and must wear a sash to visit temples will have less of an understanding of the culture than someone who spends five years living there, full-time child raisers have a greater opportunity to understand the world of childhood than parents who only have time to visit it on weekends. There is a kind of understanding that can come with direct experience that no one, even the most articulate experts, can boil down to something which can be communicated on a printed page. Child raisers who are receptive to their children, and who spend enough time in the child's world to begin to reconnect with the child within themselves, will be in the best position to begin understanding how their children see the world. From this understanding comes the ability to make the right day care decision and all the crucial decisions in child rearing.

Kids Are People Too

Where there is something strange or mysterious, preconceived notions develop. We feel uncomfortable with the unknown; we must fill the void. If parents are aware of these stereotypes, they can provide children with the care and attention that is appropriate at particular stages in their lives. They can avoid unwittingly hurting their children.

By far the strongest and most significant prejudice against children is that in the early years their feelings need not be taken seriously. This is similar to other types of prejudice.

Early American settlers believed it did not matter very much what happened to so-called primitive people, since they were only semiconscious. It would not matter to the American Indians if they had to leave their ancestral hunting grounds of a thousand years and travel hundreds of miles to live on a reservation. As shocking as it is to us now, not very long ago Europeans and Americans generally held that belief. They thought that these peoples were fundamentally different from themselves, did not possess a soul, and were subhuman.

Breaking through the prejudice against young children's feelings, Freud shocked Vienna with his novel theory that a traumatic experience in infancy and early childhood could have a lasting effect on the psyche. Since Freud, there have been great advances in the understanding of child psychology, and educators, psychologists, and pediatricians now recognize that those early "forgotten" years leave their mark. Unfortunately, this new awareness has not completely dispelled the popular notion that forgotten experiences are harmless and of no consequences to the young child. "He doesn't like going to the sitter," a supermarket checker commented, referring to her three-year-old son, "but what does it matter? He won't remember it anyway."

Adults do not remember their feelings in their earliest years, and so they have difficulty empathizing with a young child's "emotionalism." With older children and teenagers, it is quite different. The mother who remembers all too well the night her high-school boyfriend stood her up and was later seen at the party with another girl will be very sympathetic with her teenage daughter in a similar situation.

Aside from the remarkable fact that we remember very little of our earliest years, young children's lack of intellectual sophistication appears to support the notion that their emotions should not be taken too seriously. If their "emotional IQ" is roughly parallel to their obvious lack of sophistication, then they must be quite insensitive indeed. Poignant stories of childlike adults like Lennie in *Of Mice and Men*, E.T. the extraterrestrial in Steven Spielberg's 1982 film, and Charlie the idiot in *Flowers for Algernon* have beautifully expressed this prejudice. In *Of Mice and Men* a strange bond of friendship develops between two migrant laborers, George and Lennie, a mentally retarded adult. Lennie looks up to George and depends on him in a childlike fashion, and George has strong feelings of love and devotion to his friend despite his mental handicap. The story ends tragically when Lennie encounters a woman who tries to seduce him and he unintentionally breaks her neck. George finally commits a mercy killing rather than see his friend taken by an angry mob led by the woman's husband.

These stories have a strange appeal—not because most of us have had a close relationship with a mentally retarded adult, but because we were all children once. We recall or subconsciously resonate with feelings of not being understood, of being an "outsider"; feelings that we are being stereotyped and dismissed because others do not look deeply.

In this story Lennie is strange and, in a sense, primitive. Yet he is also a sensitive human being, and our initial prejudice changes to sympathy and compassion at the climax of the story. E.T., the extraterrestial being accidentally abandoned on Earth when his spaceship took off, elicits a similar sympathetic chord. He learns few English words and cannot articulate his feelings at finding himself a stranger in a strange world, but a depth of feeling lies behind his simple words, "E.T. phone home." Of course, it is the children in the neighborhood who are able to befriend and communicate with this formidable-looking "alien." Most adults running into an extraterrestrial would call the police rather than offer the strange being candy. In a way, young children are superior to adults; they do not have prejudices and preconceived notions. The other side of the coin of naïveté and innocence is the absence of prejudice and an open mind.

This open-mindedness allows children to empathize in situations where adults may have little sympathy. Butch, a four-year-old, was particularly fond of Squeaker, the pet rat. When his mother came to pick him up at our center, he ran to her, eager to share his special friend. He put the rat on her arm, and it quickly scurried up to her shoulder. "*Uck!*" Frightened, she flung it to the floor. Butch looked up at her reproachfully. "Squeaker has feelings too, you know."

People who have worked with mentally retarded children know that they often are extremely sensitive to the attitudes and emotions of the people around them. Their "emotional IQ," or ability to understand things on a feeling level, may be well developed in spite of their mental deficit. "Normal" children also are remarkably sensitive and perceptive in this respect. Yet, too frequently, their feelings are dismissed as childish or silly.

In "Magic Circle" time at the preschool program, the authors asked the children, "What can you do to make a child who is sad feel better?" The answers were a long list of distraction techniques these children had obviously been exposed to. "Give her a cookie." "Show him a toy." "Make a funny face." But when we asked the children if they felt better when someone did these things, they all emphatically said no. Although they could not express the idea fully, it was clear that when they felt sadness, it could only be modestly diminished by these offerings.

Adults often criticize young children for being upset over seemingly trivial matters. We may tune out the specter of a drowned earthworm or a bird caught in the jaws of a hungry cat. Or we may wince and turn away: "Survival of the fittest, I guess. That's the way it goes." But the same events may affect a child quite differently. As one of the authors expressed it:

> *Who speaks for compassion and gentleness*
> *Beyond the bitter chess game of success?*
> *Who is the spokesman for tenderness?*
>
> *Only the child who weeps*
> *For the fallen jay*
> *In her quiet way*
> *With her blue-grey eyes and curly hair*
> *She speaks the silent*
> *Word of peace*

Perhaps we can learn from children, and increase our awareness. Frequently, we turn off our emotions because we are trying to feel less vulnerable. This numbing process leads to an escalation of horror in the news and entertainment media, with increasingly detailed descriptions of disaster and death designed to penetrate our shell. It is a vicious circle. Exposure hardens the shell, requiring more and more sensationalistic renderings.

It is a curious thing that, in the ways in which children are fundamentally the same as adults, we have believed they were different or inferior, while adults have often failed to honor the ways in which children's experiences are unique. Parents must take the time to watch and listen to their child's inner thoughts and feelings. Once they do this, they will see what's best for their child. By overcoming these prejudices parents will respect the immense sensitivity and basic intelligence of children and will become more tuned in to their child's needs. This will guide them in making the right decision about their own child's care.

Chapter Five

Health and Your Child

Warning: Day Care May Be Hazardous to Your Child's Health

The home environment is a natural quarantine for infants and young children. When a parent is the primary child raiser, the infant's or toddler's exposure is mainly limited to the parents, perhaps a brother or sister and their friends, and an occasional playmate. All forms of group day care significantly increase the exposure of children in this age range, with large day care centers being the extreme at one end of the spectrum and day care homes with a limited enrollment lying at the other end.

In recent years outbreaks of infectious diseases in day care centers have drawn the attention of epidemiologists and pediatricians, and medical researchers have begun to study the health risks associated with various kinds of day care. While parents and day care providers might expect that infants and toddlers would trade colds and perhaps an occasional flu, recent studies reveal that the problem of day care–associated illnesses goes far beyond the common cold. The research is relatively new, and it takes time for technical knowledge to reach the general public. As a result, most parents are not aware of the health problems associated with day care.

Medical researchers now have sophisticated diagnostic tools that make it possible to probe deeply into the causes of epidemics of infectious disease. They now have tests so sensitive that the exact strain of a bacteria can be identified and this strain can be followed through the population as the outbreak or epidemic proceeds. This precision and accuracy in research enable physicians to be more accurate in their diagnosis and treatment.

With all the technological advances in the last hundred years, the old maxim that an ounce of prevention is worth a pound of cure is still true today. There remain serious diseases that continue to defy a cure or are difficult to treat or that carry the risk of serious complications in spite of prompt diagnosis and treatment. Concerned parents will gladly choose prevention of an illness over the worry and expense involved in dealing with a sick child. Are there increased risks of serious illness in day care? If so, what are the risks? What can the parent do to decrease them? Once the problem is recognized, the answer to these questions becomes a number one priority.

There is no evidence that the problem of day care–associated diseases is confined to "substandard" centers or centers in poverty areas. Appearing in the *New England Journal of Medicine* (August 19, 1982), a study by Robert F. Pass and others of the spread of cytomegalovirus (a member of the herpesvirus family) in a day care center showed that this viral infection rapidly spread through the day care center, probably through toys toddlers had put in their mouths. All the children in the center were from suburban families of middle to upper income, and yet, because of the easy spread of infection in the day care setting, these children had almost double the rate of infection of children who were cared for at home, and a significantly higher rate of infection than home-reared low-income youngsters. This is a reversal of the usual pattern, in which higher rates are normally found in low-income children.

While cytomegalovirus does not usually produce symptoms in infected children over the age of three or four months, this study illustrates how easily an infectious agent can spread in a day care environment. The oral activity of children under the age of three years is a major factor, and this occurs in good and substandard centers alike. In one study day care children under three were observed to put their hand or an object in their mouths every two minutes.

Since all the children in this cytomegalovirus study were over three months old, they were asymptomatic (medically known as a carrier state), and the researchers measured the infection rate by examining the urine for the presence of the virus. This infectious excretion of the virus (medically termed viral shedding) can go on for years after the initial infection. Interest in cytomegalovirus and how this disease spreads is not academic. Asymptomatic children are contagious, and a full-blown infection of cytomegalovirus in the first weeks of life is disastrous to an infant, with symptoms of lethargy, convulsions, jaundice, and massive enlargement of the liver and spleen. There is no specific treatment for cytomegalovirus, and it is usually fatal.

While the focus of this study was cytomegalovirus, this particular day care center was chosen because of an overlapping epidemic of a serious bacterial infection, *Hemophilus influenzae*. In the last ten years, numerous reports of outbreaks of this infection in day care centers have led to its general recognition by epidemiologists as a day care–associated disease. In this outbreak, four of the eleven infants under one year became ill with a *Hemophilus* infection during a five-month period. Technically known as *Hemophilus influenzae* type B, this bacteria is the leading cause of bacterial meningitis in children over the age of three months. It is capable of invading the brain, spinal cord, joints, and other areas of the body. The illness can be life-threatening, and most infections require hospitalization.

Dr. Stephen Hadler, an epidemiologist with the Centers for Disease Control (CDC) in Phoenix, Arizona, who has studied the problem of day care–associated diseases, explains why there is concern about group care:

> Day care centers are a fertile environment for the spread of infectious diseases, especially enterically [intestinally] transmitted diseases. Outbreaks of infections can spread beyond the centers into the families and the community.
> This represents a major potential problem in public health.

The major day care–associated diseases can be divided into two broad categories: enterically transmitted illnesses like hepatitis A and various infections of the digestive tract, and infections that begin in the respiratory system, like bacterial meningitis and influenza. (See Appendix I for a review of these diseases.) Outbreaks of infections across the country have confirmed the suspicion of a significantly increased incidence of these diseases in day care centers, and have stimulated research projects by the CDC, National Institutes of Health, and other agencies, focusing on day care centers and families and personnel connected with them.

Dr. Hadler's special interest is hepatitis A, a viral infection of the liver. A 1981 report of the CDC, part of the United States Department of Health and Human Services, outlines the findings on hepatitis. A nationwide survey showed that the spread of hepatitis within communities is often linked with day care centers that provide care for children under two years. Large centers for infants and toddlers have the highest risk of outbreaks. Preschools that do not provide care for diapered children have little risk, and day care homes with small numbers of children are also a low risk, because of the small chance the disease will be introduced. Of course, children cared for in their own home also have a low risk, for the same reason.

Dr. Hadler's interest in hepatitis led to a two-year study, in Phoenix, of 279 licensed preschools, day care homes, and day care centers. The findings were disturbing. *Two out of every three* group care arrangements accepting children under one year had at least one outbreak of hepatitis affecting three or more families. Dr. Hadler also found that, in the same area over a ten-month period, about 400 new adult cases (40 percent of total adult cases of hepatitis A) occurred in persons associated with group-care centers. Monitoring hepatitis is easier than monitoring many other diseases, because physicians are required to report new cases to local health departments. While Dr. Hadler notes that the number of cases in the area was particularly high, similar patterns of day care–associated hepatitis have been reported across the United States. Ironically, most children under three years have only minimal symptoms when infected with hepatitis A, but day care workers, parents, and older siblings can become quite ill, with weakness, fever, loss of appetite, abdominal discomfort, and headache.

Across the United States, studies (from CDC and a number of universities) of diarrheal diseases and respiratory-transmitted diseases like bacterial meningitis in various group care arrangements have shown that infants and toddlers are at a significantly increased risk of unpleasant and sometimes disabling or life-threatening illness. Scheduled for 1984, the First International Symposium on Day-Care Associated Infections will bring together hundreds of epidemiologists and other medical specialists concerned about this growing health problem. A major focus of the conference will be to begin to identify the important risk factors in various kinds of arrangements in order to attempt to control these outbreaks.

With hepatitis, it is clear that the typical pattern involves an asymptomatic, and usually unrecognized, outbreak among toddlers in the center, followed by symptomatic illness in employees and families. In Dr. Hadler's study only about 3 percent of group care arrangements with a minimum age of two or older had hepatitis outbreaks. In hepatitis — and this applies to some other infections as well — the biggest risk factor is the presence, in the group, of children under two or three years. The reasons why this is such an important factor are actually quite complex, but it is clear that the almost continuous hand-to-mouth activity so typical of children under two, combined with their being in diapers, is central to the problem. Another important factor is the size of the group. In summing up in the 1981 report, the Centers for Disease Control noted the characteristics of the high- and low-risk types of group arrangements. Infant-toddler centers, which tend to be large and accept drop-in children and have long hours, are a high risk. Preschools, on the other hand, require toilet training, tend to be smaller, have a fixed enrollment, and keep shorter hours. They are a low risk for these "day care diseases." Surprisingly, hygiene and adequacy of staffing do not eliminate the health risks, although some studies indicate that frequent hand-washing can help in controlling outbreaks of some diarrheal diseases.

Children in day care centers are at risk of developing a wide variety of infections. In 1976 an important multidisease study reported in *Pediatrics* (Anna Beth Doyle, vol. 58, 607–13) compared home-reared children and children in day care. Seven categories of symptoms were used to measure the occurrence of illness in the two groups. There was a significantly higher rate of fever, vomiting, diarrhea, respiratory symptoms, and rashes in the day care children; when only children under the age of two were compared, the differences were even more striking.

Aside from hepatitis, other enterically transmitted diseases have been responsible for outbreaks of diarrhea in day care children and their families. These are usually caused by a bacteria or protozoa, and the symptoms range from mild bouts of diarrhea and vague abdominal pain to serious illness with high fever, cramps, and bloody diarrhea. These diarrheal diseases and respiratory-transmitted diseases like influenza, rubella (German measles), and bacterial meningitis spread easily in infant-toddler centers.

Clearly, infectious diseases pose a cumulative risk to a child in an infant-toddler center. The simplest solution, in terms of the child's health, is to avoid putting infants or toddlers in group day care until they are at least three. This will not eliminate the risk, but studies suggest that it will reduce it substantially. Second choice would be a quality day care home or other arrangement limited to a few children; preferably the number of infants in such a situation would be held to an absolute minimum.

Unfortunately, the current trend is in exactly the opposite direction. The day care center for infants, toddlers, and preschool-age children is the fastest-growing type of group care arrangement in this country. Surveys show that many parents would choose center-based care over other arrangements if it were available. Because the biggest health problem in these centers (presence of large numbers of infants and toddlers) is the very thing that makes them financially viable, control will be very difficult, and the health standards will always fall short of the natural quarantine of the home environment.

In terms of contagious disease, the home setting represents the opposite end of the scale from the day care center. The small number of children and adults, particularly with today's trend toward small families, and the natural limitation of exposure to groups of new adults and children are important. Also, the length of pregnancy limits the number of children under the age of three at any given time. In this setting the newly formed immune system of the infant and toddler will mature and will function appropriately, protecting the child in future exposure to infectious diseases.

Exposure to Infection Is Not Beneficial

Since it is common knowledge that the immune system can produce resistance to a specific agent after exposure, parents often wonder if some exposure is good for their children. This misunderstanding is a holdover from the days prior to the advent of vaccinations, when certain childhood diseases like chicken pox and measles were virtually inevitable. Looking for a silver lining in the cloud of illness, parents comforted themselves with the knowledge that one disease had been checked off the list; at least their child would not get that one again. Today we have vaccines to prevent or lessen the risk of diseases such as polio, diphtheria, whooping cough, tetanus, measles, mumps, and rubella. Children can enjoy protection without actually getting sick with the disease.

In addition to this obvious advantage, there are other reasons why vaccine-produced immunity is preferable to immunity gained through contracting a disease. In the last thirty years there has been an explosion of knowledge in the medical sciences. One discovery is that chicken pox and shingles (medically known as herpes zoster) are caused by the same virus, which belongs to the same herpes family of viruses as the infamous herpes simplex (lip and genital herpes) and cytomegalovirus. Shingles, a painful infection of the central nervous system, is actually a reactivation of the latent virus that initially invaded the body as chicken pox. So the lifelong immunity from the chicken pox is an immunity against the symptoms of chicken pox, not against a later occurrence of a painful disease caused by the same virus. Even in childhood, chicken pox is not always mild, and complications occasionally occur.

Along similar lines, the measles virus has now been implicated in the development of multiple sclerosis and other serious neurological diseases. Whole measles virus has been isolated from brain specimens of patients with subacute sclerosing panencephalitis (SSPE), a progressive degenerative central nervous system disease, proving its role in the disorder. There is some evidence that vaccination in childhood may provide some protection against the development of these serious diseases. Measles is so contagious that almost all children who are not immunized will eventually become infected.

Functioning to protect the body from infection, the immune system maintains a balance with the potentially infectious and noxious agents that naturally exist in the outside environment and inside the body as well. When that balance is disturbed, the tissues of the body are invaded, resulting in infection and sometimes illness. It is very important that parents understand the distinction between infection and illness. Children may be infected and contagious but never become ill, even though their immune system has not neutralized the invasive agent.

A large number of infected children in this carrier state is the typical background for the development of an epidemic in a day care center. In one day care center that accepts children up to the age of three years, two cases of a *Hemophilus* infection, one meningitis and one infection of the facial tissues and blood, occurred where a carrier state of *half* the children in the center was demonstrated. In this study, which appeared in *Pediatrics* (March 1979), it was noted that this was in contrast to much lower rates of latent infection in four other day care centers that had not had an outbreak of *Hemophilus*, and in a control group of children not attending day care.

An infant's or toddler's resistance to infection is different from an adult's. While hepatitis tends to be a milder infection in children under three years than in older children and adults, this is not true of many diseases that threaten young children. The immune system is immature, and this lowered resistance of children, particularly under one year, makes them more vulnerable to a host of infectious agents. In addition, there are many infections that tend to be much more severe in children under one year than in older children and adults.

In *Hemophilus* infections, which can cause bacterial meningitis, the risk of illness begins to decrease after the age of three years. However, active infections before an infant reaches the age of three or four months are also unusual. This is because the newborn receives antibodies from the mother (called passive immunity) against the *Hemophilus* bacteria and these can protect the child for up to six months. This grace period occurs with a number of potential invaders.

Thousands of times a day parents across the country make decisions that take advantage of the protection of the home environment. "The doctor says Alice might still be contagious. Maybe we'd better put it off. It is too bad; I know the kids are anxious to get together to play." "My two-year-old is really sick; maybe you'd better not bring the baby over." The immune system is complex and remarkable, but there are many ways in which parents can enhance this natural resistance. Conscientious parents can greatly reduce the likelihood of illness in the under-three age group. Breast feeding, which is growing in popularity, provides the infant with anti-infectious agents present in the colostrum and breast milk that increase the infant's resistance to infection. Prompt medical attention when there is a suspicion that an illness is serious can be of tremendous value and prevent complications. When parents are concerned, they should not hesitate to contact the pediatrician for fear that the doctor might be annoyed. Recommended immunizations are beneficial. Most infants and toddlers will pass through this period without any serious illnesses. Every parent will agree that a healthy child is a real blessing.

The Day Care Center: Pressures Against Health

On the way to the day care center, four-year-old Brendan began to complain about a stomachache, but by the time he arrived at the center he seemed fine. He went right over to the block area and began to play. Barbara, a secretary and single parent, rushed out the door. Brendan's unexplained fussiness before breakfast had put her behind schedule and she was trying to make up for lost time. Barbara had just settled in at her desk when the telephone rang with a most unwelcome message: Brendan was not okay. He had just vomited all over the block area. Was he running a fever? No, but he seemed listless and wanted his mommy. Barbara told the center she would call them right back and immediately phoned Connie, her "backup." Connie was usually home and had agreed to help out if Brendan was ever sick. No answer. Mr. Fitch, the senior partner, put a file on Barbara's desk. "I'd like this right away," he said, raising his eyebrows. Barbara couldn't understand his attitude; this had happened only once before. It wasn't as though Brendan was sick all the time. The phone rang again. It was the center. One of the day care workers wanted to know if Barbara could come right over. "I just can't come right now. Can't you have someone take care of him for a while?"

In the world of working parents and full-time day care, a sick child presents a vexing problem that taxes the patience of employers, day care personnel, and parents alike. With parents depending on ten hours a day of continuous care, an infant's or child's sudden illness puts parents under tremendous stress. Appearing in the February 20, 1979, issue of *Family Circle* magazine, a survey of three thousand working women showed that the potential of a child's becoming ill was a major concern. Two out of three said that their only option was to stay at home themselves. While day care centers have a major risk of infection "built in" because of age and size factors, the lack of adequate alternatives when a child becomes ill results in sick or contagious children attending centers and compounds the potential health problems inherent in the day care situation. This vicious circle results in outbreaks of infectious diseases that affect the health of parents, siblings, and day care personnel as well.

Monday morning ten-month-old Stephen seemed active and healthy, but that night he was lying in a hospital crib, with intravenous tubes supplying his body with an electrolyte solution of sodium and potassium that he badly needed to combat the dehydration and acid-base imbalance caused by severe diarrhea. Because the metabolic rate and exchange of bodily fluids are much more rapid in children than adults, dehydration poses a serious threat to them and must be corrected immediately. Monday evening, while returning home from the center, Stephen suddenly began shaking uncontrollably, and when he reached home his temperature was 103°F. He pulled his knees up with cramps, and his mother was shocked to see diarrhea containing blood. She bundled him back into the car and sped to the emergency room. Stephen was admitted. The doctor explained that Stephen had bacillary dysentery and began asking questions. Did Stephen attend a day care center? Did he come in contact with any children who were sick or had diarrhea? Stephen's mother resented his question about day care. She had heard that there had been a few cases of diarrhea at the center, but she felt she had no warning that something like this would happen.

This physician's interest in the background of the case was appropriate. Bacillary dysentery, also known as shigellosis, is a highly contagious bacterial infection of the digestive tract, and it is mandatory for doctors to report each case to the health department. Shigellosis is a serious illness, particularly in children under two years of age, and there is a significant mortality rate in very young children if prompt hospitalization and supportive care are delayed.

Reports of day care center–associated outbreaks of shigellosis have been received by the Centers for Disease Control from all over the country: New Hampshire, Virginia, Washington, D.C., Ohio, Kentucky, Texas. Because of problems in detection and reporting, it is difficult to know the exact number of families that are affected each year. In one screening, it was estimated that only about 60 percent of the discovered cases in the study area would have been picked up by the existing case-reporting system. But one thing is certain: increasing numbers of outbreaks of shigellosis in day care centers since 1972 are a clear indication of a significant health problem.

The problems in controlling the spread of dysentery in these epidemics is typical of difficulties health officials face in the control of day care–associated infections. In one outbreak, a child attending a day care center developed diarrhea. Three days later his five-year-old brother also developed diarrhea and attended the day care center while ill. Twelve other children at the center became ill. In another center, a day care worker became ill and initiated an outbreak.

Faced with such an outbreak and the responsibility of protecting the community, health officials frequently consider closing the day care center. But the economic and social impact on parents and day care directors and employees is substantial. This is frequently a point of controversy. "How can they ask me to close my center?" asks Ethel, a director of a center with fifty-seven children ranging in age from three months to five years. "All the parents will think the center is responsible. We will lose all our enrollment!" she protests. Parents operating on tight schedules are not exactly overjoyed at the prospect either. Even if their child is not ill, they must quickly find alternative arrangements, perhaps another center.

This becomes part of a widening circle of problems in controlling the initial outbreak, according to a 1981 CDC report. Infected children who are asymptomatic are put in other centers due to a closing or because of parents' concern that their child might become infected in a center that obviously has a problem. This, of course, spreads the disease to children in the new center, day care workers, and families, and so it goes, on and on. In addition, health-department officials do not have the right to require treatment of an infected child, or to require participation in screening tests to check for the presence of the disease or tests to monitor the spread of an epidemic over a period of months.

If the center is not closed, health officials may recommend that parents *not* remove their child from that center, so as to avoid the spread to other centers. From the parents' point of view, the request that they keep a child, who is not obviously ill, in a center with a known outbreak of a contagious disease like *Shigella* infection or hepatitis seems unreasonable. In desperation, some of the parents will not go along with the health department's recommendations, hoping that by switching from the affected center their child will escape infection.

In cases where most parents choose to follow the recommendations for treatment, it still may be difficult to control the outbreak. Some parents may feel that treatment of a child who is not obviously ill (carrier state) is unreasonable. A few parents may refuse treatment for their child, and shigellosis is so contagious that a single untreated case can start a new chain. Another problem is that even after symptoms have subsided, those infected can continue to be contagious for several weeks. And in diseases like hepatitis that have a long incubation period (two to six weeks), substantial spread of an infection may occur before an outbreak is detected.

In terms of hygiene and procedures at a center, specific health-department recommendations may put a practical and economic strain on the center: constant hand-washing and washing of toys, disposable plates and towels, separate sinks in bathroom, kitchen, and diaper-changing areas, paper-towel dispensers at each, isolation of sick children, and careful attention to personal hygiene of each child. With an already overworked and poorly paid staff, compliance is naturally quite low.

In all the day care–associated diseases, financial pressures affect not only day care centers, but health departments as well. In a January 1983 editorial in the *Journal of the American Medical Association,* Dr. Stanley Schuman of the Medical University of South Carolina notes that there are usually inadequate funds for proper enforcement of regulations regarding day care centers. Health agencies are not immune to budgetary cutbacks and the trend toward deregulation. In center outbreaks requiring antibiotics, and extensive and repeated laboratory testing, the issue of payment by the "private versus public" sectors is still unresolved. In general, "bottom-line" cutbacks result in cuts in health standards across the board.

Another major problem is financial pressures on day care workers themselves. "When one teacher was sick, we didn't get a substitute. There wasn't any money for that. So whoever was there had to deal with all thirty kids. I dragged myself in sick lots of times knowing what the other workers would go through that day if I didn't," says a former day care worker from New York City. Exposure works both ways between day care workers and children, with the possibility of spread to the children's families and to the day care worker's family as well. Day care workers typically receive very low pay, have inadequate sick leave, and have no health coverage provided. The result is that sick staff members will frequently show up for work at the center.

The pressures day care workers feel apply to working parents as well. Although nearly all day care programs have rules requiring parents to keep sick children home, there is great pressure on the parents to keep the child in the center as much as possible. Most programs do not give refunds when a child is absent, and sitters who can stay home with a sick child are expensive and hard to find. The majority of employers do not offer "parental sick leave" for parents who wish to take care of their sick child.

Current medical science has a formidable armory of medications and procedures to combat day care–associated diseases, but total prevention of these illnesses and of outbreaks occurring is still out of reach. Preventive vaccines or medications for the diarrheal diseases and for most upper respiratory infections (except immunizations for the "childhood diseases" like measles) do not exist. It is possible that a preventive vaccine for hepatitis type A may be developed within the next five to ten years, but for the time being reducing exposure is still the primary method of prevention for these diseases.

Although the pressures on day care providers work against control of the spread of center-based outbreaks, current knowledge does not support the idea that poor hygiene alone is responsible for initiating outbreaks of most day care–associated illnesses. Poor hygiene within a center does not create or introduce an infectious agent; only an infected person can do that. As a result, as mentioned previously, the health problem of day care centers is not confined to substandard centers and outbreaks cut across all socioeconomic boundaries. Large numbers of young children spending long days together is still the primary cause of day care center epidemics.

Chapter Six
Early Childhood Education

The Development of Early Childhood Education

Early childhood education in Europe and the United States has developed over a period of roughly a hundred and fifty years and represents a gradual growing awareness of the nature and needs of preschool-age children. Prior to the nineteenth century, learning that took place before a child entered elementary school was the province of the family. By the nineteenth century, the concept of a nursery school had emerged, but the idea that preschool-age children were really capable of significant learning grew slowly from the 1920s to the present.

The earliest preschools stressed moral development. In 1816, Robert Owen, a Scottish cotton mill owner, opened a "preparatory school for infants" of his employees. Children from ages one to six attended this school, which had an emphasis on play. No formal lessons were given; rather, the purpose was to "prevent children from acquiring bad habits, to give them good ones, and to form their dispositions to mutual kindness."

Friedrich Froebel, a German educator, demonstrated that children could learn through play, without formal instruction. In 1837 he opened a school for young children in Blankenburg, and in 1840 he coined the word *kindergarten,* literally translated as "children's garden." He wanted to convey the idea that children, like plants, should be tended but allowed to grow freely.

Gradually nursery schools changed from a place where children could learn through play to a formal academic environment. In England in the last part of the nineteenth century three- to five-year-old children attended strict schools where they were required to sit at desks for long hours reciting lessons and learning reading, writing, and arithmetic. They were forbidden to socialize, and there was little provision for physical activity.

There were few nursery schools in the United States at the turn of the century. Colleges first began to set up programs to train teachers to work with preschool children in the 1920s. During the Depression and World War II the federal government provided funds for the care of children under elementary-school age, but it was not until the 1960s that there was an upsurge in interest in the educational possibilities of preschool.

By the sixties, educators were beginning to view early intellectual stimulation as an important element in the development of intelligence. Educational psychologists believed that the course of a young child's life could be altered significantly by early learning experiences, and nursery schools with a traditional emphasis on play and art projects were criticized. A new cognitive emphasis emerged in nursery schools, and the word *nursery,* with its connotation of babies, was put aside in favor of the label *preschool.*

With this strong feeling that the child's early intellectual development would have an effect on later schooling, the federally funded Project Head Start was introduced in 1965 to give economically and culturally disadvantaged children an opportunity to learn basic concepts prior to entering elementary school. The goal was to give these children a head start that would improve their level of performance when they entered school.

Today preschools represent very diverse attitudes toward teaching academics, with some programs teaching reading and others believing strongly that nursery school is a place for social experience, art activities, and learning through play. Kindergarten is not compulsory in all states, but in states that offer a kindergarten program some preschool directors express a feeling of being pressured. "We never used to do so much with letters and numbers," a California preschool director told a prospective enrollee's mother apologetically, "but the kindergartens in this area expect it, and we'd lose our enrollment if our kids didn't measure up."

Whether they learn at home or in a preschool, children today are expected to enter kindergarten with certain basic concepts and some facts at hand. A kindergarten-readiness test includes the concepts of loud and soft, light and heavy, big and small, less and more, as well as expecting children to count and to be able to name body parts, colors, and shapes.

Beyond the occasional extremes of preschoolers that have no program other than unstructured free play for the entire morning, and schools that represent a kind of reactionary strictness and a preoccupation with academic drills, the majority of preschool programs currently attempt to combine periods of unstructured play with more structured activities ranging from puzzles and music to reading readiness and science projects. Most child psychologists agree—and, unlike the day care issue, there is a consensus on this point—that preschool-age children from about three to kindergarten age benefit most from a program that includes activities aimed at affective and cognitive development; that is, emotional needs and socialization, and learning activities. What is not clear is the line between play and learning activities when you are talking about preschoolers.

Play and "Serious Learning"

All the varied forms of a young child's play have a "purpose," in the sense that these activities are stepping-stones in the child's development of more and more sophisticated skills. In biological terms, these activities are an "adaptation" in order to develop skills necessary to function in the environment. But it is absurd to propose that the infant or toddler has an awareness of this, or any other "purpose." The child building a block tower is not thinking, "This will be excellent preparation if I should decide to become a structural engineer."

Because adults are very goal-oriented, questions naturally arise about what the right kind of activities to promote academic achievement are. Some preschools claim educational programs designed to provide those essential activities without which a child's development might be slowed or blocked. Toys and games are sold with packaging and advertising claiming that these items are educational and provide the necessary experiences for intellectual development. "Educational and fun too!"

Some parents have the idea that a child's mind is like a computer: the right buttons must be pushed in the right sequence, or the computer will not operate. Developmental psychology has indeed concluded that there are important physical and intellectual stages in a young child's development, but research has also shown that human intelligence develops in response to hundreds of thousands of different experiences in the early years. The development of intelligence is extremely complex, and a child's mind is very open and flexible. A rigid approach to learning is unnecessary; if anything, it blocks the natural tendency to exploration, which is so important. Some books imply that infants' development will be slowed if parents fail to put stimulating balloons on the ceiling and mobiles over the crib. Of course, one has only to look around the world to realize babies thrive with no official toys at all. Children in developing nations are well coordinated without having used balance beams, and they learn to hold pencils without having played with knob puzzles.

Even if regimentation and rigid learning systems produced intellectual geniuses (and they don't), there remains the fundamental question as to whether children have the right to be themselves. The recent history of education in the U.S. has seen dramatic swings from "free schools," where children create their own curriculum, to "back to basics," with a strong emphasis on the "three R's." If pure play and fantasy and imagination are natural elements in the world of the child, then should ideas of progress and utilitarian philosophy squelch this process?

Robert Frost said, "Too much form, too little fire." Young children need a certain amount of freedom, a balance between structured learning activities and pure play. Perhaps the learning psychologists are only half right about the developmental function of play. Maybe there is another purpose. Perhaps experiencing the sheer joy of play is also important to the child's development and adjustment to the world.

Unfortunately, the recent trend toward full-time day care in the United States has dramatically affected traditional preschools throughout the country. Responding to the demand, some preschools are now offering extended day programs that run from 9:00 to 2:30 rather than 9:00 to 12:00, and large numbers have become hybrids that have a preschool program in the morning and a day care–type program for the rest of the day. This is a step backward in the historical development of early childhood education. Until the day care problem emerged, preschool education focused more and more on a respect for and recognition of the intelligence and learning potential of each preschool-age child. In trying to meet parents' need for a custodial arrangement for their children, converted preschools are succumbing to the pressures of full-day group care, with its necessary emphasis on regimentation and the consideration of group over individual needs.

More Is Not Better

As the use of all types of day care grows, more and more children are spending their time in day care centers or at preschools that have been "converted" to full-time day care. Working parents often have concerns about putting their children in these centers, and the day care industry has responded to this concern by assuring parents that full-time day care is in fact an educational experience that enhances their children's development. This is a half-truth. Full-time day care has no educational benefits over a morning or afternoon preschool program, but it can have a very negative effect on children's emotional development.

Children under two years nine months (which is the typical minimum age for enrollment in preschool) are learning all the time, and a parent who has had some training in early childhood education, or has taken some parent education courses, is in the best position to enhance this process for children in this age group. A very young child will enjoy and learn from the experience of playing with the parent and will gain much from parental encouragement and responsiveness. There is no educational advantage to starting children under the age of two and a half to three in a day care or preschool-type program; most parents are quite capable of learning all they need to know to guide their child's cognitive development in the first three years.

Three- to five-year-old children are ready to benefit from the educational and social experiences a good half-day preschool program with trained teachers can provide, but more is not better. A full-day preschool program would not be an improvement. There is a good reason for preschool programs, even kindergarten, being traditionally a half-day program. Children's capacity for structured or concentrated learning activities in this age group is very limited. Many day care centers are purely custodial, and even in those few day care centers that really do have an educational component with trained teachers, these activities typically take place as part of the morning program. The afternoon involves lunch, a rest time, and some free play. Day care workers themselves often realize that children have a limited attention span and a limited capacity to concentrate. One director of an afternoon day care program at a preschool told of her dissent with the board of directors. "I fought to keep the day care program in the afternoon recreational. The kids needed time to sit in the sandbox and dig a hole for a whole hour if they wanted to." If adults consider whether they would learn twice as much taking ten college courses a semester instead of four or five, they will understand this. Even if a student's adviser were to permit such insanity, the student would soon discover that all his or her courses were suffering from such an overload.

Alison Clarke-Stewart's Chicago Study of Child Care and Development (which was reported in her book *Daycare*, Harvard University Press, 1982) compares the cognitive development of day care center and home care children (children who are home with parents or a sitter or in a day care home), and suggests that preschool children who regularly attend a program outside the home, whether it be preschool or full-time day care, tend to do slightly better at knowing color names, counting, and so forth. According to Clarke-Stewart the measured educational benefits of attendance at a day care program were found to be about the same as the measured benefits from attending a half-day preschool. In other words, the very studies of cognitive development that the day care industry and day care advocates proudly point to strongly suggest that full-time day care has absolutely no educational benefits over the much more limited separation of half-day preschool.

Also, it should be noted that as an average, the slight gains reported for preschool and day care children over stay-at-home children are not lasting. Studies by William Fowler, Nasim Khan, and others show that the "advantage" evens out by the early grades of elementary school. However, as discussed in Chapter 1, the emotional damage of full-time day care begun at an early age does not go away by third grade; its effects can last a lifetime.

Most studies of low-risk children from relatively advantaged families have failed to show any difference in intellectual development between day care and home-reared children (for example, Moncrieff Cochran, *Child Development*, 1977, vol. 48, 702–7). Day care or preschool is considered particularly beneficial for "high-risk" children from disadvantaged families, and the New York City Infant Day Care Study (report published by the Medical and Health Research Association of New York City, 1978, Golden and Rosenbluth, et al.) results suggest that this benefit is not limited to enrollment in university-based programs. Where parents are doing little to contribute to the development of their child's verbal and reasoning skills, and are not encouraging children's learning by reading stories or other activities, the difference between day care or preschool and home care children is particularly marked. However, it is important to realize that some of these same gains for high-risk children may be achieved through intervention in the home situation.

Dr. Phyllis Levenstein, director of the Mother-Child Home Program of the Verbal Interaction Project in Freeport, New York, has found that two- to four-year-old children from low-income families benefited as much or more from an in-home educational program as did disadvantaged preschool or day care children who attended programs outside the home. In contrast to the trend to take low-income children out of the home to prevent the home situation from having a negative influence on the child's development, Dr. Levenstein believed that if children were taught at home the family would be strengthened *and* the child would make cognitive gains. She found that low-income mothers were cooperative and willing to extend themselves on their children's behalf and, contrary to the stereotype of the low-income family, were capable of providing the elements essential to a young child's cognitive development.

In the Mother-Child Home Program, a toy demonstrator visited the homes twice a week over a seven-month period, each time bringing a book or toy designed to stimulate verbal interaction between the mother and child. The demonstrator modeled techniques for using the materials but did no formal teaching, and left the material with the family. In third grade the children in this program, who were mostly black and Hispanic, were at the national norm in reading and arithmetic scores, scoring significantly higher than children in control groups. This project suggests that even "disadvantaged" mothers can be teachers for their young children, and that cognitive gains are no justification for putting low-income children—or any children, for that matter—in full-time day care. Parent education combined with a quality educational half-day program may be an excellent choice for these high-risk groups. The emotional advantages of home care need not be sacrificed.

Learning and the Whole Child

There is general agreement in the field of child development that parental expectations and parental behavior profoundly affect learning and the development of competence. Dr. Levenstein realized that parents would be in a unique position as teachers for their preschool-age children because of the close attachment. All that is needed is for parents to understand that there is a tremendous potential for them to be a teacher for their young children and some simple guidance for the parents about appropriate methods and materials. While a quality morning or afternoon preschool program, three to five days a week, can be a very enjoyable, educational, and stimulating experience for a preschooler, parents should realize that there is much teaching they can do themselves and the preschool experience is not essential to their child's intellectual development.

However, if their children are to get benefits similar to those they would get from a quality preschool experience, parents need to learn something about activities appropriate to this age group—there are many fine books available—and must be sure that their children's needs for peer contact are met.

Many of the child raisers the authors interviewed felt that their children had more creative abilities and were capable of more independent thinking than children who had been "raised in day care." "It seems to me that perhaps my children have been exposed to more concepts, phenomena of nature, mathematical concepts, prereading and reading skills, and so on," says Kathy Tannenbaum, a former special-education teacher who is staying home to raise her three children.

Ruth Cohen finds her six-year-old son is "more interested in the world at large, more able to perceive the subtleties that only a close relationship of constant exchange with an adult can give—like perception of art, music, history, nature, and religion. Not just rote learning of these things, but subtle perceptions leading to independent thinking."

And teachers have reported similar observations. A Midwest kindergarten teacher thinking back on all the children she'd taught said, "When I think of the ten worst—worst in terms of cognitive and social development—I find a mix of day care and home care kids. But when I think of the ten best kids I ever taught, none of those came from families where both parents worked."

Studies and experiences of group care, from around the world, support these anecdotes and suggest that this negative effect on creativity and independent thinking is a real phenomenon. In Israel, a small percentage of the population live in kibbutzim where children are raised in groups and spend little time with their parents. Noted psychologists such as Bruno Bettelheim, Erik Erikson, and others have compared kibbutz children with Israeli children raised in families, and many researchers agree that there is a kind of sameness in the personality of the kibbutz children, an absence of individual elements that are important in creative intelligence and independent thinking. In school achievement tests, kibbutz children score in the middle range; the kibbutz experience has eliminated the lowest scores, but it has also failed to produce children who score as high as children raised in quality home environments.

In the Soviet Union, a similar problem has developed, and government-run group care, particularly for very young children, has been the subject of internal criticism. Dr. Benjamin Spock, in his book *Raising Children in a Difficult Time,* speculates that one of the reasons the government is no longer pushing group care for very young children is the discovery that these children failed to develop the ability to think creatively.

While it is true that, *on the average*, full-time day care children and preschool children score about the same on competency tests, the observations and studies concerning creativity and independent thinking indicate that, for the individual child, particularly a child with above-average intelligence or special creative abilities, full-time day care can have an adverse effect, stifling creativity and discouraging independent thinking. On the other hand, a part-time preschool experience allows children to have a lot of time away from the group—time to initiate their own activities, and to explore the world at their own pace, in their own way. Children need private time as well as social experiences to fully develop their creative abilities. The artist, the theoretical physicist, the composer, the novelist, and the sculptor all tend to work independently and alone. While they all "stand on the shoulders" of others who have gone before, any original contribution they make is, almost without exception, an individual achievement, not a product of a cooperative group effort. Freud, Einstein, Stravinsky, and Picasso all represent creative genius that was intensely personal and individual, and was a breakthrough unlike what had gone before. Yet, cumulatively, the contribution that individual "independent thinkers" have made throughout history has profoundly affected the course of civilization.

It is not surprising that all children need time away from the social pressures of the group, time to "be themselves" and thus fully develop their creative potential. The pressure to conform exerted by a group on the individual child is substantial and has been studied by psychologists. Group ostracism is a fierce thing for anyone to face, and a three- or four-year-old is not likely to resist for very long. Rather than be faced with such a confrontation, it is much better for preschool-age children to have enough time away from the group to establish their own sense of themselves and their personal likes and dislikes. Obviously, group care forty to fifty hours a week does not satisfy this need.

In addition to the potentially adverse effect full-time day care has on children's creative intelligence, day care interferes with parents' opportunities to transmit their values to their children. Young children develop their own value system by observing and interacting with adults; they assimilate most of their values from their primary attachments, usually their parents. Greatly decreased contact with the parents limits the parents' ability to transmit their values and convictions to their children. Role models are very important to young children, and in this, actions speak louder than words. Merely telling children what behavior is expected is only a small component in the larger constellation of experiences that become the base for children's values. Just as with bonding, there is no such thing as "quality time" in the sense of somehow instantaneously instilling parental values and ethics in young children. Learning values is the product of countless hours and thousands of experiences.

When we look at the whole child—cognitive development, emotional needs, physical development, and need for moral guidance—it is important to recognize that these aspects are not really separate. Each affects the others, and the trend in early childhood education, and educational psychology in general, is to acknowledge this relationship. Parents who choose to be child raisers, full time or part time, are in a unique position; because of their close relationship with their child, conscientious parents can simultaneously support their child's cognitive, emotional, physical, and moral development.

Child raisers who assume the teacher role with their preschool-age children almost always find the experience stimulating and rewarding. The child and parent both enjoy and benefit from this kind of interaction. By the time their child is one or one and a half years old, the parents can shift gears from being mainly observers in the learning process to actively participating in teaching and guiding their child. By the time their child is four or five years old, parents will be surprised to find that the child is capable of asking very difficult questions, questions that remind us how little we know about so many things or reveal how much of what we take for granted is really arbitrary and cultural. "Why does the Earth spin?" "Where do people go when they die?" "Why can't I eat with my fingers?" "Do birds have bladders?"

As parents learn about how young children learn, they begin to understand the complexity of the process, and the child's "firsts" take on a different meaning. A child's first steps become the beginning of a succession of firsts relating to the gradual development of balance, coordination, and agility. Child raisers watch firsts in learning and physical development that are happening very frequently. This coordinated succession of developmental steps is really quite remarkable, and it underlies all of our adult abilities.

Preschoolers are very receptive and curious, and parents, depending on their knowledge or inclination, can teach cooking, crafts, music, foreign languages, math, science, reading readiness, or reading, using appropriate activities adjusted to their child's age, interest, and attention span. It doesn't take special abilities or training for parents to be able to do this—just enthusiasm and some activity guides and reference books for ideas. Trial and error will quickly reveal which activities are a "hit," which are not, and why. And parents who decide to send their child to a preschool program, which in general is first choice for four- and five-year-olds, can still supplement that experience with broadening experiences and activities that are not available or possible at school, in addition to continuing with learning activities on an occasional basis.

Child raisers who actively participate in these activities with their children, whether they utilize a preschool or not, are both caring for and teaching their children; and this can be a very rewarding experience for the parent and a very beneficial experience for the child as well. Part-time or full-time child raisers who are actively involved as parents and teachers are relating to the whole child—to their child's cognitive development, physical development, emotional needs, need for moral guidance. It is in this role that parents can truly give the most to their children.

Chapter Seven

What's Best for Your Child

Society has long recognized that children have different needs at different stages of their development. It is no coincidence that the State does not require children to start school before they are five years old. The traditional kindergarten is a half-day program designed to introduce children to the school experience in a gentle and part-time manner. Educators have long felt that children need the consistency and security of a single teacher for their first years at school. It is not until junior high school or high school that students start to study different subjects with different teachers, and even then the idea of consistency is maintained by having a *home*room teacher.

Based on our experience as preschool teachers and day care workers, we have arrived at a rule of thumb to help parents decide how much separation a child can comfortably handle on a daily basis. We recommend a maximum of one hour a day for each year of age up to the age of five. Most two-year-olds can comfortably spend two hours a day away from their parents, and five hours is fine for most five-year-olds. Ideally, a baby should be home with a parent until age three and then start a morning preschool for three hours a day. The hours of separation can be increased until first grade, at which time most children can accept the idea of a full day's separation from their parents. The number of hours a day the child spends away from parents is much more critical than the number of days a week. A three-year-old will usually adapt easily to three hours a day, five days a week, but will probably have a much harder time with the same fifteen hours of separation divided into two days of seven and a half hours.

Unfortunately, some parents find themselves in a situation where they have no choice about taking a full-time job and putting their babies in day care if they are to eat and pay the rent. The most these parents can do is realize that inevitable does not equate with beneficial. Understanding that the situation is not good for their children may make them feel concerned, but that concern can be a motivating force in making them take action to get themselves and their children into a better situation as soon as possible.

When day care is a necessary compromise, a relative who lives close by may be the most satisfactory substitute for care by a parent. Of course, if Grandma has back problems and cannot lift the baby, and Great-aunt Gertrude is so forgetful she can't keep track of her keys, let alone an active toddler, then parents will have to search for alternatives. But a grandmother or other relative who is able and willing to take on the care of a child is likely to care more about the child than anyone who is simply hired for the job. For older and retired people it is a way to be useful and productive. A relative who feels appreciated is more likely to stick with the job than a hired person.

When this is not possible, we recommend an in-home sitter for the first three years. This gives the children the chance to feel special in the early years, and to be with someone who can watch them grow and show genuine enthusiasm about each milestone. A day care worker watching the 225th child take her first step can't get too excited. Also, as we discussed in Chapter 5, there are significant health risks associated with group care of children under three.

If group care is an absolute necessity, the smaller the size of the group the better. A day care home is preferable to an infant center healthwise, and if the ratio of babies to adults is the same, a *good* day care home is also emotionally first choice.

From about age three, children begin to crave social experiences with other children. They are also ready for many of the activities a preschool has to offer. (It takes a very dedicated grandma or nanny to permit messes like finger painting or splatter painting!) If it is possible for children to attend a morning preschool program and continue care with Grandma or the same sitter in the afternoon, this is a good arrangement. A day care home for the afternoon would be another viable alternative if the day care mother can pick the child up from preschool.

For children over three, day care homes do not have an advantage over centers. The merits of the particular home and center in question need to be weighed. However, for health reasons, centers that accept infants and toddlers as well as three years and up should be avoided.

Six-, seven-, and eight-year-olds are usually emotionally ready for a full day's separation from their parents, but they are *not* ready to spend unsupervised those three or four hours between the time school gets out and the time parents get home from work. Children this age need after-school care, and are ready to enjoy a variety of extracurricular activities. The increase in after-school day care centers run by schools, park and recreation departments, and private business is a very positive trend, since children this age are too immature to be safely left alone.

If parents of elementary-school children can manage to work three-quarters time, or can arrange flexitime schedules so they are home when their children come home from school, this is ideal. Although children may sometimes only touch base before going out to play, knowing a parent is home so they can discuss a concern promotes a secure feeling. By the time they reach fifth or sixth grade, children tend to spend less time with their parents as they become more independent and learn to cycle or take public transportation to after-school activities.

Of course, parents often are not comparing apples to apples when deciding on substitute care. The toddler's parents must weigh a mediocre home sitter arrangement against a good day care home, or a four-year-old's parents must choose between a lonely situation with a great sitter and a social situation in a mediocre day care center. At best we can give guidelines to be used, along with parents' good sense, in evaluating a specific family situation.

All full-time day care should be viewed as a compromise, to be used only when it is absolutely necessary or on a temporary basis until satisfactory arrangements with less extensive separation can be worked out. When avoiding extensive separation from their children is top priority, parents may manage to create a child-raiser role for themselves where at first there seemed to be no alternatives. In the following chapters, we will discuss the problems facing child raisers and the ways in which child raisers are handling the dual responsibilities of work and parenting.

PART TWO

The Parents' View

Chapter Eight

Pressures on Child Raisers

Aside from financial pressures, and concerns about reentry into the work force, mothers and fathers who are considering being or have chosen to be child raisers often face peer-group pressures and personal psychological issues that discourage such a choice. It is primarily these psychological issues that will be discussed in Part Two, while economic and political issues will be discussed in Part Three. Sometimes parents are shielded from these forces because their immediate circle of friends and family is supportive of their values and their choices, but very often this is not the case and parents receive much subtle or not-so-subtle criticism, or even open hostility. In addition, traditional roles of the father and mother are changing, and a great deal of confusion and sometimes even bitterness have been left in the wake.

In the midst of this upheaval, women child-raisers may receive criticism from the women's movement, and male child-raisers feel pressure from a society that still operates on a macho value system in which men can *either* be strong and tough *or* caring and a "pushover." Even when two-paycheck families find ways to balance wage-earning and child-raising responsibilities, these social and psychological elements do not disappear. It takes adjustments and some self-knowledge and insight into our societal values in order to be able to really enjoy the role of child raiser.

Pressures on Fathers

> *I have a handsome baby son,*
> *A little boy so fine.*
> *And when I look at him, I feel*
> *The whole world is mine.*
>
> *But seldom do I see my child*
> *When he's awake and bright.*
> *When I leave home, he's still asleep,*
> *When I return, it's night.*
>
> *I look at him in anguish then,*
> *I know it seems so clear—*
> *When once again my child awakes—*
> *His Daddy won't be here....*
>
> Translated by Ruth Rubin

This song of a sweatshop worker was written in 1887, but the anguish parents can feel when the need to work takes them away from their children has not changed. The father describes his pain at being a stranger to his own child. His wife tells him of all the child has done, the bright things he has said, but such tales only make the father sad; if he cannot see his son himself, his life is empty.

Although many fathers today want to be involved in their children's lives, and to be more than the traditional aloof breadwinner and disciplinarian, financial pressures and unsympathetic employers do not make this easy. Paternal leaves of absence are rare indeed. A San Francisco advertising executive describes a life that does not allow him much more contact with his one-year-old daughter than the sweatshop worker of a hundred years ago had with his child. "I leave for work in the morning before she's up because I have a one-hour commute. I'm never done at five. I get home eight, nine, sometimes even eleven at night. Sometimes I don't see her awake for days."

Employers are often not even willing to accommodate fathers who want to be home for a special occasion. A thirty-three-year-old sales manager who had attended natural-childbirth classes with his wife eagerly looked forward to participating in his child's birth. He requested that he not be sent out of town during his wife's ninth month. He was extremely bitter when the request was denied and he was sent on a ten-day sales trip. "I missed the whole thing. I didn't even get to see my son until he was ten days old. And my wife wanted me there at the birth and in the days that followed. But what was I going to do? Quit and be out of a job just when I had new responsibilities?"

Although fathers often mention sorrow at missing a specific event like the child's birth, or first laugh, or first steps, they can feel the loss every day. "I miss her when I'm at work," the father of a ten-month-old girl admitted. "I can be involved in working on a complex computer program, but an hour never goes by that I don't think of her four or five times. I wonder, 'What's she doing now? Is she playing, is she napping, is her mother taking her out in the stroller?'"

Many fathers feel social pressure that prevents them from spending available time with their young children. They feel obliged to hide indoors or in the back yard lest someone think they are "weird." "Where I live, a father just doesn't take his baby for a walk in the stroller," complains a father from Great Falls, Montana. "It's like I can't be seen with my son until he's old enough to hold a baseball bat or a fishing pole."

A Los Angeles father of a six-month-old girl who is sharing child care with his wife finds pressure has made them divide the responsibilities less evenly than they had anticipated. "My wife can do errands with the baby in a backpack and everyone says, 'Oh, what a cute baby,' but I get such bad vibes when I go to the lumberyard or the auto-repair place, I've given up. If she cries everyone looks accusingly, and if I sing her little songs or do things like my wife does to keep her happy then I really get strange looks. The only way I can do it is if I pretend I'm really put out about it—like my wife is sick so I have to do it—but if I let on I'm enjoying it, forget it!"

Fortunately, most fathers who choose to be child raisers do not let macho social pressures stop them, but they do often try to hide their "socially unacceptable" role. And there are many fathers who will not consider actively sharing in the care of their children because there is still so little precedent for such a role. Men who realize that caring and sensitivity are compatible with strength and independence will not be stopped by these macho stereotypes, but as long as these persist, such men will continue to be annoyed and angered by them. One thirty-two-year-old attorney from New York City complained, "I'm sharing care of our daughter and I'm surprised how much I'm enjoying it. But I feel a little like Christopher Columbus. I wish there was more support."

Flight from Intimacy

> *I am a rock, I am an island.*
> *And a rock feels no pain.*
> *And an island never cries.*
> Paul Simon

In contemporary America, social pressures and important psychological issues combine to create a trend toward rejection of intimacy and long-term commitment in interpersonal relationships. And this affects our attitudes about closeness between adults and our attitudes about closeness between parents and children as well. A high divorce rate, mobility, violence, alienation—all have left their mark, and a flight from intimacy has seriously damaged interpersonal relationships in our society. Many men and women who have been divorced find it difficult to really trust a new relationship, and people find themselves caught in a whirlpool of decreasing expectations.

Sometimes people have responded to this erosion of trust and closeness by a reaffirmation of closeness in their relationships, but others have chosen to "adapt" by withdrawing into a world where closeness and giving are not important. A number of pop philosophies such as est and the "new hedonism" have evolved to justify and rationalize this withdrawal, and there has been an increasing glorification of personal pleasures and personal triumphs in an attempt to prove that "looking out for number one" is the true road to happiness and personal fulfillment.

Although most parents still seek closeness with their children, this flight from intimacy is one factor that has made the idea of full-time day care more acceptable in our society. In the extreme case, parents sometimes totally reject closeness with their child. The idea that dependence is a sign of weakness is applied to the child, who is, of course, physically and emotionally dependent on the parents. If the parents feel uncomfortable in being "emotionally available," they may compensate by teaching the child that being tough, independent, and isolated is the best way to be. They believe they are fulfilling their obligation to the child by preparing him or her for the "hard, cold reality" of the world. The following dialogue is based on an actual conversation.

Child: Where's my sandwich?

Mom: I made a sandwich for myself. You'll have to make your own sandwich.

Child: Why?

Mom: Because you're your own person.

Child: So?

Mom: So you have to learn to do things for yourself.

Child: But I already know how to make a sandwich.

Mom: Look, I've had to look out for myself in this world, and you've got to do the same thing. If you don't look out for yourself, who'll look out for you?

Child: But I am looking out for myself. That's why I want a sandwich.

Mom: You don't understand. It's not good to be dependent on other people. It's my job as your mother to make sure you face reality. Reality may not be fun, but it's the only one we've got.

Child: But Jenny's mom makes her sandwiches.

Mom: But Jenny's mom won't always be around. Someday Jenny will be by herself. She won't always have a mommy to help her. That's why you have to start learning to do things for yourself now.

Child: You used to make me sandwiches.

Mom: I'm very tired. That's because I used to think that was my job. If I didn't I would feel guilty. I don't feel guilty anymore. There's no reason for anyone to feel guilty because they're looking out for number one. Everyone is just looking out for themselves anyway.

Child: I'm not hungry anymore.

Children are profoundly influenced by the attitudes of adults. This mother's idea of "reality" is determining what will be. By not acting in a caring way toward her child, by assuring him that "that's the way life is," she will raise a child who will not care for her. She will increase her own isolation and find some bitter comfort in the mistaken idea that that's the way it is for everyone.

Mark Twain warned, "We should be careful to get out of an experience only the wisdom that is in it—and stop there; lest we be like the cat that sits down on a hot stove-lid. She will never sit down on a hot stove-lid again—and that is well; but also she will never sit down on a cold one anymore." This mother was in a relationship where the person she was depending on let her down. In compensation she developed a "self-protectiveness" and a generalized negative view of closeness and giving. She came to the false conclusion that all stoves are hot and is passing this on to her child in the name of "reality." Her idea of reality comes from her own bitterness.

This kind of emotional withdrawal has sometimes resulted in parents encouraging their children to be independent prematurely. In *EST: 60 Hours That Transform Your Life* (Harper & Row, 1976), a book authorized by est founder Werner Erhardt, Adelaide Bry recounts the story of two parents, both est graduates, who sent their eight-year-old son to an est seminar. After finishing the seminar, the child came to the conclusion that he didn't really need his parents. His mother agreed. She was, of course, encouraging him in an illusion. An eight-year-old usually cannot make his own way in the world, and when war or other disasters force a child to grow up instantaneously and assume the burdens of an adult, there is a psychological price to pay. Young children are dependent on an adult to fill their physical and emotional needs. They cannot look out for themselves.

When children are old enough to take on additional responsibilities, it may ease their parents' burden, but there is no way to hurry a child toward greater independence and responsibility without this acceleration's taking its toll. When parents want children to grow up fast because they feel too drained emotionally to take on the demands of nurturing a child, the children feel the strain.

It is important for children to learn to be responsible and to be as independent as makes sense for their level of maturity. But it is also good for children to learn that doing something for someone else can make them feel good, and that letting someone do something for you is *not* a sign of weakness.

Many parents like preschools where the children learn to be responsible and independent. "They learn to hang up their coat and wash their hands and scrub the table." However, this worthwhile goal can become distorted. The authors were with a preschool teacher one day as the children were leaving school. One little girl handed a rolled-up painting she had done to her mother as they walked to the car together. The teacher was disgusted. "Look at that! That child is perfectly capable of carrying her own picture, yet the mother lets her get away with that irresponsible behavior."

The teacher's assumptions were all wrong. She assumed that you do something only for someone who is incapable of doing that task alone. Doing something for someone can simply be a sign of acceptance, affection, or love. When a husband makes a Sunday pancake breakfast for his wife, it is not because he believes she is incapable of doing it herself. He simply enjoys doing something for her, and she appreciates it. Her own pancake-making ability doesn't atrophy as a result.

Because being a caring parent and child raiser involves a considerable amount of hard work and "self-sacrifice," the "new hedonism," with its attendant pop philosophies, raises issues about giving and taking, child raising and day care, altruism and selfishness. It is easy for child raisers to feel intimidated by people who suggest that altruism is an old-fashioned idea, because few of us like to be accused of being old-fashioned in our approach to child raising.

The philosophies and pop religions of the late sixties and the seventies spouted many New Age "golden rules." "Do your own thing." "Be your own person." "Look out for number one." Fritz Perls's gestalt prayer says, "I do my thing, and you do your thing. I am not in this world to live up to your expectations and you are not in this world to live up to mine." This was not intended to apply to a parent-infant relationship. But it raises an important question: what responsibility do parents who bring a new human being into the world have? Someone must fulfill a child's physical needs if a child is to live. Someone must fulfill the emotional needs if a child is to thrive.

Robert Ringer, author of *Looking Out for No. 1* (Fawcett, 1978), assures people they don't need to live up to "ought to's." No one can tell other people what is right for them to do. He urges people to get rid of anyone in their life who causes them discomfort or complications. This attitude can be extremely destructive to children and to the parent-child relationship. "I don't mind giving up my child's first steps. With my son in day care, I have control over my life. Freedom feels good to me," says a twenty-seven-year-old journalist who put her six-week-old son in full-time day care. In a healthy parent-child relationship, the needs of parent *and* child must be balanced.

Looking out for number one assumes that people live in vacuums. Although lip service is paid to the idea that you shouldn't forcibly interfere with the rights of others, nothing is said about hurting people through *not* taking a certain action. For example, Ringer claims that no one has the right to tell him to conserve energy. His energy consumption is his own business. All anyone has the right to do is conserve energy themselves. Such an attitude ignores the fact that we are all living on one planet, with limited resources. If the "number ones" squander energy, the rest of us will have to live near nuclear power plants that might otherwise never have had to be built, and to see the last of our wild rivers dammed. There are very few actions a person can take that truly affect no one else.

The basic problem with the looking-out-for-number-one philosophy is that it ignores the fact that we are all social beings living in this society. Responsibility and guilt are not just "old-fashioned morality" but relate to the basic trust necessary for peaceful social interaction. Women's liberation, looking out for number one, est, and other philosophies have all in their own way questioned the validity of social expectations, and yet the fact remains that without expectations and obligations of any kind the social fabric would be torn beyond repair.

A genuine closeness with children should be based on an honest altruism, not role expectations and social pressures, but the new hedonism has gone too far, reacting against stifling social conventions and insincerity in empty words and rituals. We should not throw the baby out with the bath water. What is needed in parenting, and in all relationships, is a new altruism grounded in honesty and self-understanding.

Emotional withdrawal is not the answer. The antiromanticism of the women's movement rejected the Hollywood romance with cardboard people and an ever-present bowl of cherries. That is well and good, but it does not follow that intimacy and giving in interpersonal relationships cannot exist once our two-dimensional stereotypes are replaced by a more complex perception of human beings as they really are.

A return to intimacy, to giving and closeness in interpersonal relationships, is essential to the well-being of our society. This is why day care is not a women's issue, or even a children's-rights issue. The whole of society must recognize the problems of day care and find a way to create a climate hospitable to caring and family life.

Chapter Nine
Pressures on Mothers

Women's Liberation

> *"The hardest part about full-time parenting is the low esteem a segment of the women's movement has placed on nurturers who are unpaid. What a rotten thing for women to do to each other!"*
>
> Maria Martinelli, mother of three
Auburn, California

In the past many homemakers felt that men did not fully appreciate what went into raising children and running a household, but they often received understanding and support from other women. Today mothers who choose to be child raisers find it particularly disturbing when other women criticize them.

It is very unfortunate that the women's movement has attacked the homemaker and child-raiser roles, and there is now only the beginning of a recognition that a serious mistake has been made. When women denigrate the status of child raising and homemaking it can only intensify the existing prejudice against this non-job-related role.

In the initial stages of the women's movement the housewife role became the symbol of society's belief, held by both men and women, that women were not capable of mastering male-dominated occupations like medicine and law. The traditional attitude was that women simply did not have what it takes. In their anger and shock in clearly seeing this prejudice, women sought to prove themselves in the work world without stopping to consider the tremendous importance of the experience of child rearing for children and for parents.

Today many women enter the work world not just for financial reasons but for personal satisfaction and in order to prove their abilities to themselves and others. Many parents do have a choice between the prestige of work outside the home and a higher standard of living or full-time or part-time child raising, and some make a choice that compromises their children's needs.

Three-year-olds at the authors' center often had a keen sense of what was important in *their* life. We heard Billy and Barry's mother say, "Mommy is working so we can take nice vacations and go skiing. You want to go to the snow, don't you, Barry?" Barry was not beguiled. With pain in his eyes he said quietly, "No, Mommy, we'd rather have you."

Paul and Maria Martinelli are clear about their priorities. Maria left her teaching job when their first child was born, and does not plan to return until their youngest is school age. Paul is an elementary school teacher and works as a house painter in the summers in the heat of California's Central Valley in order to earn the extra three thousand dollars a year they need to keep Maria home with the children. Though money is tight, Maria is pleased with how things have worked out. "When my half-grown daughters recall their early years they recall interactions, not whether our furniture was from Breuner's [an exclusive furniture store] or whether their mother's clothes were in fashion for the seventies. My husband and I want the same good things for our new baby."

The goals of working outside the home and receiving equal pay for equal work are not incompatible with taking a child care leave for several years. Once society recognizes that women are capable of mastering a full range of types of work, including jobs like auto mechanic and surgeon, there is no reason for a woman to feel embarrassed about taking time off to raise her children. In reacting against the housewife role many women looked at their mothers and said, "I'll *never* do that." A growing number of working women are now beginning to feel the lack of family experience, and to realize that child care leaves and part-time work have the potential to fulfill that need without compromising the gains of the women's movement.

Rather than rejecting the part-time or full-time child-raiser role, we should raise its status so that both fathers and mothers can fully participate in the parenting process with dignity and self-respect. Mothers badly need to feel that they can raise their children without acknowledging that they are somehow inferior or have a lack of commitment to their job. So far most of the spokespeople for the women's movement, Betty Friedan being the notable exception, have only paid lip service to what Friedan calls "unfinished business" and have not made raising the status of the role of the homemaker and child raiser a priority on their agenda.

However, a reevaluation is under way in the women's movement, and hopefully this will soon spread to a serious consideration of the importance of parenting and the family experience. Betty Friedan, in *The Second Stage* (Summit Books, 1981), questions adopting masculinism and success according to the male model. A major reevaluation of the materialism and one-upmanship of our society is needed so that child raising is afforded equal status with employment or a career. The assumptions of our highly competitive culture, with the accompanying overemphasis on job status, must be corrected so that children and family life will not get shortchanged.

Mothers, and fathers for that matter, will be able to enjoy staying home and making granola, baking bread, and playing games with their children without feeling embarrassed or ashamed when the homemaker and child-raiser roles are given the status they deserve. An overemphasis on status interferes with these family roles, and as Dr. Benjamin Spock points out in *Raising Children in a Difficult Time,* this imbalance will be corrected when outside jobs are judged more by the satisfaction they give than by their pay or prestige. Once the importance of the child-raiser role in the emotional development of young children is recognized, parents who take that role will get the support and respect they deserve.

Tinker, Tailor, Soldier, Sailor, Housewife

> *"When people ask me if I work I say 'yes,' sixteen hours a day at home and 'on call' at night. They raise their eyebrows a bit in disbelief until I tell them all the things I do."*
>
> Terry Franklin, *mother of four*
> Nicasio, California

There is a double standard when it comes to deciding what is work. A homemaker who cleans house and prepares meals for an elderly person or a child has a valued skill, for which she receives a paycheck. But a housewife and child raiser is considered unskilled, and may even have a hard time convincing anyone she works. Despite the word "house*work*," no one really takes a woman who cleans her own house seriously. A maid works, but a housewife is just a housewife.

Women who are at home deeply resent the way some segments of society view housewives. Every woman we interviewed agreed that there are people who stereotype housewives and mothers. Barbara Leung, a mother of two from Glen Rock, New Jersey, put it this way: "What really raises my blood pressure is commercials on TV which give the impression that we spend our time looking at how white the wash is or how shiny the floor is." Kathy Tannenbaum gets mad when people ask, "Do you work?" "I'd love to say, 'No, I just lie around and paint my nails and eat bonbons. And now and then I have to run out for more movie magazines, between soap operas.' Usually I say something like 'Yes, I work like crazy at home.'"

We have no word for the woman who gets married and quits her job, the mother who is at home with little ones, and the wife who stays home and chooses not to take a job after all the children have married or gone off to college. Joanne Deschamps, who stayed home to take care of her two sons, likes the term *child raiser*. "The name child raiser sounds good but it is not commonly used. Society stereotypes *housewives* as the most boring things on earth. Housewives are thought to be empty-headed, unglamorous, always looking sloppy and tired and bored. A prostitute would sound much more interesting and less embarrassing."

When working women put their children in full-time day care many have lingering doubts and feelings of guilt. This unresolved guilt is frequently a basis for feelings of hostility against full-time child raisers. Ruth Cohen is a nurse's aide in Ashland, Oregon, who stopped working when her son was born. Her own mother's death when she was one and a half years old forced her to spend her childhood in foster homes, and she was determined to give her son the loving childhood she never had. Ruth sees people who criticize housewives as lacking in self-awareness. Her insights into the contempt with which some career-minded men and women view full-time child raisers made her feelings of anger change to pity. "It's really too funny and sad. The people who put down child raisers cut themselves off from the love they always wanted to receive and be able to give by this sort of defense. I can't be mad at such self-ignorance."

Most child raisers we interviewed agree that urban areas and university towns put the most pressure on women to "do something more," and that childless professionals and working mothers are the most critical of them. The fact that the publishing industry is centered in urban areas, and that many editors are working mothers, may account for some of the strong, "back to work" bias on the part of many women's magazines.

Many magazines are concerned about making their readers feel guilty. When they do defend the homemaker role, the response is often angry. Judith Nolte simply asked in her October 1980 editorial in *American Baby*, "Why have so many women fallen into this trap in the first place; into thinking that ... they must join the movement out of the house and into the job market; that being a secretary or a nurse is somehow better than being 'just a mother'?" She received a barrage of letters, which were published in January 1981 under the heading "Working Mothers Strike Back." One was from a mother who complained, "Why can't your magazine print articles on how to find capable sitters or handle a job and a home instead of unwittingly adding to a working mother's guilt?" Another was an angry letter from a nurse who asserted emphatically that being a nurse *was* more important than being a mother.

Raising children is a joy, but it is also work. Mothers who work part time outside their home are in a particularly good position to compare the demands of the two jobs.

"I get angry when I hear people say that work outside the home is harder, more stressful, more creative, etc. It drives me crazy when I hear men say they need to relax after a hard day at work and expect the wife to provide this space for them. It is as if they see the wife as goofing off all day. Since I work both inside and outside the home, I know that child rearing is by far the harder and more demanding," asserts Robin Kaufman, a hospital-unit manager with a one-year-old son.

The Grass Is Greener: The Myth of the Happy Worker

There are days when moms know only too well that housework and child care are work. The morning a mother drags herself out of bed at six A.M. to give the three-year-old breakfast when she was up until four in the morning with the colicky new baby, and the first thing she does is step in a mess the dog made on the rug because that new medication the vet prescribed has given him diarrhea—well, that morning the Chinese idea of twenty-four-hour day care sounds great, and the idea of being able to walk out and catch the eight o'clock bus while leaving a sitter to deal with it all is a pretty appealing second choice.

A job appears to have immediate, measurable awards. There is a paycheck to assure workers each week that their skills are valued, and there is the possibility of approval from co-workers and supervisors for a job well done.

Women who choose the housewife-mother role feel they are giving their children something more than the working neighbors, yet they are often shy about speaking up because they have no yardstick to measure "better" or "happier" children against. Just as people in the job world are respected or looked down upon according to their professional status and their salary level, with little regard for their capacity to be centered or loving human beings, children are usually judged by how well they do in school or in sports. A full-time mother rarely gets any praise if she lists as her accomplishments "I raised two children to be loving human beings." But a working mother who uses part of her income to dress her children in designer clothes and buy them lots of toys can expect to hear people comment, "What a good mother she is!" Again, the materialism of the culture comes through in valuing what is visible, obvious, and easily measurable.

The kinds of jobs that most women who look for employment will find are not the glamorous jobs they have read of. Once the excitement of the first paycheck wears off, many women find that being a secretary or a clerk is actually less stimulating and has fewer rewards than raising children. But even if women were to receive better pay, they might not be happier. In the Soviet Union, where the majority of women earn as much as or more than their husbands, more than one million couples were divorced last year. The Soviet newspaper *Kirgizhia* attributes this to the stress of combining a home with an outside job.

In the United States, although the number of women in the work force has more than doubled in the last thirty years, women are not happier than ever before. Studies (as reported in *Unfinished Business: Pressure Points in the Lives of Women*, Maggie Scarf, Doubleday, 1980) show that the rate of depression in employed women is just as high as in women who stay at home. And a survey of top career women showed they drank and smoked as much as men, suffered equally from "male diseases" like heart attacks and lung cancer, and had a shortened life expectancy similar to a man's. The stress of balancing job and family responsibilities can cause accidents as well. Stress related to child care problems is reported to be a factor in industrial accidents of women assembly-line workers in the auto industry, and this is probably true in other industries as well. So full-time work is not really an answer for most mothers. Increasing the status of child-raisers and making child care leaves and well-paying part-time work available would greatly reduce the stress of having to choose between full-time mothering or a full-time career, or unsatisfactorily combining the two.

In some cases, depending on the number of preschool children and the husband's income bracket, working does not even make financial sense. Joanne Deschamps, a bilingual secretary and translator who is married to a CPA, left her job when her first child was born. "My husband and I both agreed it would be too demanding physically and mentally for me to work outside the home. Financially we figured out that it would hardly be worth it after paying taxes, baby-sitter, transportation, work clothes, etc."

Over half of all married women who work full time could afford to work part time if such work were available. A Houston computer programmer figured out that she would actually save money by working less. "We do takeout a lot. I buy convenience foods and end up shopping at expensive convenience stores because they're the ones that are open late. By the time I get around to sending an item in for repair the warranty has run out. I would come out *ahead* if I could work four days a week."

A recent survey showed that 89 percent of women who worked outside the home felt that their work and family life interfered with each other. Although some husbands are willing to help out at home, the majority of husbands do not share equally in homemaking and child raising. For many women, working at a paying job simply means having two jobs.

The Supermom

> "Being a housewife has been the most demanding job I have ever done. To work full time on top of that seems to me like sheer slavery—the woman who does that juggling act is anything but liberated."
>
> Joanne Deschamps, mother of two
> Mill Valley, California

Angela Gonsman, a Montessori preschool director with two young children of her own who left her job because "I was a nervous wreck trying to get everything done to a reasonable level of existence," finds many benefits in staying home. "There are meals on time," she explains as she kneads a loaf of whole-wheat bread that will be coming out of the oven as her husband arrives home from work, "and good balanced ones. There is calmness when we are all together, not running around getting groceries."

Jobs are demanding. Children are demanding. But the skills required to achieve success in the working world are quite different from the skills required for good parenting. Jobs stress efficiency. Workers look for ways to cut corners and save time. But in dealing with young children the efficient thing is often *not* the best thing for the child. It may be efficient to prop a bottle in the baby's crib at feeding time and wash the dishes while he or she drinks—but the baby will miss out on the close personal contact that goes with being held during feedings. Hugs, tickles, and smiles are all an essential part of a healthy baby-parent relationship—but they cannot be done efficiently! A parent must be able to operate at a slow enough pace to relax and enjoy the baby without feeling the need to evaluate the cost-benefit ratio of every bounce on the knee or toss in the air.

"When you work your mind is in a different time space; with children you *must* go on a slower time level," explains Angela. A few women have reserves of energy and patience that enable them to work full time an still be warmly mothering when they come home at night. But many more, who could be quite patient and understanding mothers if they were insulated from the strains and drains of the working world, find themselves snapping at their children as they pick them up from day care.

The media has fostered the myth of the Supermom who can be a success in her full-time job, pick the kids up from day care smiling, prepare a quick, nutritious, economical meal that will please even the pickiest eaters, patiently help the older ones with homework, read the younger ones a story, and still have time to herself to read *Forbes, Time, Ms.*, and at least one best-seller a week. She keeps the house spotless without help, throws four-course dinner parties on the weekend, makes the kids' clothes, and plays a good game of tennis.

Working women who find that the laundry is piling up, the mending has overflowed the sewing basket, and they are relying on the Colonel for dinner for the fourth time that week often feel that they are at fault. It is the Supermom myth that is bunk. Homemaking and child-raising are a job—and not every woman can handle two jobs even if she does have a husband who likes to cook and is willing to do the dishes. To try to live up to an unrealistic ideal is frustrating and can send self-esteem plummeting.

Child raisers who are considering going back to work and mothers who are running themselves ragged trying to "do it all" can see through the myth of the Supermom once they understand how it originates.

When women take jobs because they want to work, or because they need to work, they do not feel comfortable with the idea that day care might be harmful to their children. A number of rationalizations have emerged to help women overcome the natural concern they feel at leaving their children for ten hours a day. A few women say, "It breaks my heart every day when I drop my baby off at day care," but many more find such honesty too painful. The denial mechanism is strong enough for them to buy these rationalizations. (We should point out that many of these same rationalizations are used by men as well.)

Here are some of the common ones.

Rationalization #1: *It's quality time that counts.*

The quality-versus-quantity debate is a false dichotomy. Obviously, what is best for children is a lot of quality time. Though not all stay-at-home mothers give that, it is *impossible* for any working mother to give her children a lot of quality time. But even if the choice were one of a tiny bit of high-quality time or a large amount of lower-quality time, quality time could not win out. Children can thrive on good-sized portions of rice and beans and corn, but they will soon starve on one bite a day of filet mignon.

Of the hundreds of children who passed through our care, the authors never heard *one* say that the quality of time in any way made up for their loss. Although mothers often said they were happier working, and that this made the quality of time they spent with their children better, we typically saw scenes like this:

Carl's mother arrives at 6:00 P.M., tired and frazzled. Carl tries to show her a picture he has painted.

"Show me later. Get your lunch box. Come on." She is already halfway out the door.

Carl trails after her, crying at the rebuff and at the effort of trying to balance his painting, his lunch box, his fire engine, and the cup of fruit salad he made in a cooking project that afternoon. We can tell from his mother's mood what sort of evening Carl will have. So much for the precious two hours he will get to spend with his mother between leaving day care and going to bed.

Working parents sometimes try to compress into the evening hours those activities they did with their child before they got a job. "Let's see, how many stories a day did I used to read her? Three? Then I'll still read her three stories. Then nothing will have changed." But to a child an hour with Mommy is still an hour with Mommy, and eight hours in day care is still eight hours in day care. A single hour cannot be expanded by stuffing many stories and activities into it. To a very young child a few hours with a parent will always be experienced as much less than many hours.

Because parents are so activity-oriented, they tend to rate time spent "doing things" with their children as constructive and ignore the rest. "What with cleaning, shopping, and cooking I really only played with him an hour a day anyway." What that mother does not realize is that to a young child her presence, even in another room, makes a big difference. The experience of building a block tower in the living room knowing Mommy's in the kitchen *is* very different from the experience of building a block tower in the house alone or with a sitter in the next room. It may feel the same to the mother to cook dinner with her child out of the house or playing in the next room, but to her child the ability to touch base makes all the difference in the world. When children feel they are being cared for by that special person, the feeling determines the quality of their experience no matter what activity they are engaged in.

Rationalization #2: *Kids of stay-at-home mothers are burdened by smother love.*

"My mother would have been so much better off if she had worked. Since her only satisfaction derived from what my father and my sister and I were doing, she became overbearing. I don't want to be that way with my children, so I'm going to put them in day care as soon as I have them."

This woman is remembering a mother who had never gone out to work in her life. Once she and her sister were grown enough to be busy with their own activities, the mother had nothing to do with herself, so her restless energy interfered with their lives.

But a typical three-year-old would be happy to have Mommy and Daddy play games all day and never get tired of it. Young children are sponges and will absorb as much energy as anyone wants to give them.

This woman's story is an excellent reason for a mother not to stay home *all her life*, but does not apply to staying home until a child begins to naturally be more independent. Some people have a tendency to make things black-or-white—a mother is a working mother or a stay-at-home mother. The authors do not recommend that a mother stay home for eighteen years. That is clearly unnecessary and does not benefit either the mother or the child. But a parent can give a child a good start in life by staying home or working part time in those first years. This woman does not even remember those early years, which were so important. She thinks only of the interfering mother of her last twelve years at home, years when probably her mother *should* have been working, or at least should have developed some outside interests.

Rationalization #3: *I couldn't teach my child all those things.*

Knowledge is power. School is great. The first symptom when someone has fallen prey to this syndrome is the casual announcement, "Oh, I have to pick my son up from school now." You think of her eight-month-old son, do a double take, frantically search your memory for some older child you've forgotten, and finally realize she means she's got to pick the baby up from day care.

Even the best infant care centers, the ones with personnel trained in early childhood education, cannot teach the babies anything more than their parents could. Toddlers enjoy many activities, and are certainly learning all the time. But there is no magic in the way a child care worker sings a song, rolls a ball, or reads a story. Children will learn just as much if they do these activities at home with a parent.

Even in a day care center for preschoolers much of the children's time is spent in routine activities. It doesn't take a master's degree in early childhood education to supervise a snack, a rest time, or play in the playground. Parents do as much all the time.

But what of reading readiness? And numbers? Don't children learn those things, and doesn't that take some skill to teach? In a program that is educational rather than simply custodial, three- to five-year-old children certainly can learn numbers, letters, basic science concepts, and much more. And it does take skill to teach those things. But that is no reason to send a child to day care. This is an excellent reason to send a child to an educational preschool for three hours a day, several days a week. As we discussed in Chapter 2, studies are often misleading because they compare children who stay home full time with full-time day care children. Children could get the same benefits these studies claim by attending a half-day preschool.

Rationalization #4: *I believe peer contact is important so I send my child to day care.*

Peer contact is important. But for a young child it is not as important as contact with a parent. It is an excellent reason to send a child to preschool. It is *not* a reason to send a child to day care eight or ten hours a day. Prolonged contact with groups of other children can be frightening and confusing. Mom and Dad and brothers and sisters are the center of a young child's life. Contact with *them* is crucial.

Rationalization #5: *I'm sending my children to day care so they will be independent.*

Every mother wants to be the mom of the child who gaily waves good-bye at the kindergarten door, and is afraid of being the one with the fearful, tearful child clutching at her skirts. Some parents think the solution is "get 'em used to it early."

Suppose two mothers got wind of Joseph's prediction that there would be seven good years followed by seven lean years. The one fed her baby as well as she could during the good years. The other decided she'd better get her baby used to hard times, and gave her very meager portions. When the lean years struck, the undernourished child was the first to succumb, while the child who had been well fed in her early years survived the hardships of the lean years.

You will not find this story in the Bible, of course. But you will find it all around you. The children who are nourished by love feel secure and have the easiest time when the "famine" of separation hits. But the children who have been deprived since infancy have no reserves to fall back on.

True, children who have been in day care since they were six weeks old may not wail at the kindergarten door. They have long since discovered this is useless. But their lack of nourishment will be evident all their lives, especially when they try to form a close loving relationship with another human being.

The foregoing rationalizations may provide some comfort for working mothers, but the right decision for the mother and child must be based on a correct understanding of children and their needs, not false assumptions.

Children Are the Future Society

In spite of feeling that their commitment to full-time mothering is often misunderstood, many child raisers *are* finding their role rewarding. Tessa Dinkeloo Dimin, an Ossining, New York, mother of three who is staying home for a few years, expressed what many child raisers feel when she said, "If I am happy, if I find life fulfilling and rewarding, then I am a success."

Many of the mothers the authors interviewed saw through the current myths and stereotypes and made a conscious decision to be child raisers; some until the youngest reached school age, others for a longer period of time. Mothers of babies often spoke of the joy of nurturing new life. Robin Kaufman looked at fourteen-month-old Max and said, "My rewards are seeing my son happy, his spontaneous hugs and smiles, watching him discover the world around him and in turn rediscovering the simple joys around me."

Kathleen Galt-Theis, an Ohio mother of two, whose husband, Joe, now shares child care while she works part time as a waitress, said, "I feel rather strongly that for me to develop as a whole individual, full-time parenting was an important part of that process. To give to someone so completely, without thoughts of any return, is such an honor. Although it does come back one-hundredfold with hugs, thank yous, and a sense of love so complete and unadulterated, I feel honored to be able to experience parenting and share their lives."

Mothers of older children spoke of the satisfaction of feeling that their children were turning out so well. In interviewing stay-at-home mothers the authors met many sensitive, caring boys and girls from preschoolers to teenagers. Joanne Deschamps's sons were two of them. "I know that I can give my children the time they need from me. My children's teachers have always given me so many compliments about my boys, always saying that they are a joy to be around, that they are well adjusted. I cannot help being proud."

Women who had tried working after becoming mothers and then stopped felt released from guilt and enjoyed their children more than ever. Angela Gonsman, who left work partly because she felt her preschool son was finding day care stressful, told us, "I am doing something I know in my heart I should be doing. I don't feel guilty as I did before, when I was working part time. Ultimately to me love does make the world go round. A child fed on day care from a disinterested party will lack that intimate caring that will nurture him in a deeper and more nourishing way."

Some mothers compared their own closeness with their children to the kinds of relationships they saw working neighbors have with their children. Terry Franklin is a special person not only to her own children, but to others in the town as well.

"What has been most rewarding about full-time parenting? Sharing the daily joys and concerns of the children which occur spontaneously and at unpredictable moments. Being there to answer questions when they arise. Being a friend to my boys' friends. I am one of the few moms at home, and therefore a part of afternoon plans and bull sessions—all the kids come to our house. I'm available to take them all to practices and cheer them on in soccer, basketball, and baseball. It's fun!"

Some stay-at-home mothers have been criticized for putting energy into their children rather than the world at large. Such critics have a narrow view. Parents who love and spend time with their children are giving their children the capacity to love and care about other human beings. They are doing an urgently needed job. These stay-at-home mothers have a powerful effect on the society as a whole. Children are the future society, and it is our hope that they will grow up to serve the cause of peace on our planet. Children who grow up to join the ranks of the isolated and alienated cannot help this cause. A mother who truly understands the importance of these issues can say proudly, "I am doing something important. I am a mother, a homemaker, and a child raiser, and a good one at that."

Chapter Ten

Overcoming Doubts About Being a Child Raiser

Perhaps somewhere there is a mother who never doubted that staying home with her children full time was the best thing for them and for her. If so, we never found her. All the mothers we interviewed had at some point had questions in their minds, and most had done quite a bit of soul-searching before deciding that staying home with children was the right thing to do. Even after making the decision, doubts often continued to surface. "Am I doing the right thing? Did I make the right decision?"

In some ways the problems of a mother at home are similar to those of a retired person. There is a feeling of no longer being an actively contributing member of society. There is no supervisor to say, "You're doing a good job!" In short, there is potential for an identity crisis.

There are many concerns and difficulties, both real and imagined, that push women toward the decision to put their children in day care and return to work. Boredom, loneliness, anxiety about spoiling the child, and financial pressures are all problems that seem to have as their simplest, easiest solution getting a full-time job.

These concerns seem to reach a boiling point at various stages. The first crisis comes when maternity leave is up. "If I let this job go, will I ever get another?" The second time the pressure cooker tends to explode is around two years and nine months, when a child is old enough to go to a nursery school with an extended day program. This is a good time to think of enrolling a child in a half-day preschool program. Although full-time day care is not advisable, children at this age can really benefit from being with teachers trained in early childhood education, and they usually enjoy nursery school. Mothers, after three years at home, are often looking forward to having some time to themselves in the morning. When money is tight, many communities have co-op schools, which are less expensive than other nursery schools and have the advantage of providing the opportunity for women to meet other mothers. The third time women usually start eyeing the want ads is when the youngest child reaches first grade. At this point there is no need for a mother to resist if that is what she wants to do. Almost all first-grade children can handle the idea of Mommy working as long as they had sustained intimate contact in the first years. Mothers who choose to go to work full time at this stage can do so knowing they have given their children the best possible start in life.

Although the number of male child-raisers has increased, fathers still represent a tiny fraction of all full-time child raisers. Just like female child-raisers, they face financial pressures and the uncertainties of reentry, but there are many concerns and psychological pressures that are unique. In this chapter the authors have deliberately focused on specific concerns expressed by mothers, because this is the predominant situation. We deeply regret that this is the case. Many men still have a tremendous reluctance to actively and directly share the child-raiser responsibilities, particularly for very young children.

The traditional breadwinner role for the father remains essentially intact even though there is an increase in fathers' participation in the process of pregnancy and childbirth, and a growing number of fathers are expressing an interest in spending more time with infants and toddlers. We feel greater involvement is a positive trend, and believe greater participation is beneficial for both fathers and children. Indeed, a father's participation is essential for many of the work arrangements outlined in Chapter 13, which avoid the need for full-time day care and which can help alleviate some of the career and financial pressures on today's mothers and fathers.

Loneliness and Isolation

Most girls growing up in the last decade have been exposed to the image of the lonely housewife wasting away in suburbia. The big event of the day is opening the door when the mail carrier comes. He or she hands her the mail and she says, "Thank you," relishing the only two words she will speak to an adult until the six o'clock train pulls in. Finally her husband arrives, but instead of engaging in the stimulating conversation she so much craves he puts up his feet and disappears behind a newspaper to "unwind."

The days of coffee klatches, of sharing gossip with a neighbor while the kids all play under the big old apple tree in the back yard, are disappearing. That neighbor is likely to be working, and her kids are off in day care.

The mobility of today's society adds to feelings of isolation. By the time a woman is ready to become a mother she may no longer be living in the town she grew up in, and former schoolmates and siblings may be far away. Today, unlike the fifties and sixties, even in the suburbs people's social life tends to revolve more around co-workers than neighbors. A job often seems like the only reasonable avenue of meeting people.

Fear of loneliness is a concern of many pregnant women who plan to quit work and become full-time mothers. It is made worse by the very natural feelings many women have of wanting their baby to be part of a family and a community. An apartment building where neighbors wouldn't recognize each other if they passed in the street suddenly seems impossibly cold. Mothers-to-be find themselves missing family members living far away, though they were quite content with holiday visits until this time.

Housewives may feel they are taking on the loneliest job on earth, but feelings of isolation are not the special province of the child raiser. Conditions that keep a mother and baby indoors (extreme weather, unsafe streets, poor public transportation, and so on) also affect seniors and the handicapped. Isolation is the lot of the author, the artist or craftsperson, and others who work at home. People who work outside the home may also feel starved for social contact. The salesperson in a small store, the night guard, the meter attendant may not speak to a soul for hours on end.

A mother at least can look forward to company. That infant staring off into space will one day very soon feel like a real little person in the house. Although there is a need for adult companionship, it is hard for a mother to feel lonely when little arms are wrapped around her neck and a little voice is saying, "I yuv you, Mommy."

Leaving the job may make a woman feel isolated in some ways, but having a child brings her closer to people in other ways. As the pregnancy becomes visible, many women find it to be an icebreaker. Other women on the street, on the bus, in the supermarket will stop to talk, to ask, "When's the baby due?" The taboos against talking to a stranger break down around a pregnant woman. The taboos also break down around children. Few can resist peeking into a baby carriage. Taking a baby to a shopping center is a very different—and much more sociable—experience than shopping alone.

Children gravitate toward each other. Mothers gravitate toward each other. Many women find they increase their social circle with the contacts they make through their children. If a mother is fortunate enough to live in areas where there are natural meeting places, that is a real help. "The city parks have other women like me too," notes Maria Martinelli, a mother of three who plans to return to teaching when her youngest child reaches school age. "I just study who's there, their children, and then try to strike up a conversation. Usually the other person is *delighted* to be greeted." In other situations women must make more effort to search out or form mothers' groups, to find activities for the under-three set.

Jenny Ross has found a number of activities she and her baby both enjoy. "We go swimming, and to toddlers' gyms, and two mothers' groups during the week. Contact with other people, especially mothers and babies, is very important to me!"

Because contact with other people is so essential for a new mother's well-being, it is important for couples to plan for it whenever possible. "A car at my disposal has helped me the most," says Cathy McAllister, a full-time child raiser living in a small town in the Sierra foothills. If a car is not a possibility, the couple may at least want to live in an area close to public transportation and try to budget for one class or special activity each week. Living in an area with sidewalks (or streets that are wide and not too busy) will make a big difference. And of course, if at all possible, avoid bringing that new baby home to a third-floor apartment in a walk-up.

If a couple is considering moving before the baby arrives, there are ways to check out a neighborhood even in a strange area. Visiting the parks during school hours will usually tell whether there are other mothers of young children in the neighborhood. In areas where most mothers work, the parks will be empty until school lets out. It is often helpful to check the local newspaper, the Y, the community center, and the local college for activities for babies and their mothers.

Boredom and Bananas

A twenty-eight-year-old family counselor from Colorado had a beautiful home birth with her husband present. But when her daughter was six weeks old, she decided to return to work. "I'd go bananas if I stayed home with her," she said.

Child raisers often hear childless women and working fathers and mothers claim they'd "go bananas" if they stayed home with children. The interesting thing about men and women who say they would go bananas is that they rarely say it wistfully, or apologetically as if admitting a failing in themselves. Sometimes they are not admitting a failing; they are boasting. When workers tell child raisers that they would go bananas if they stayed home with their children, they may be saying, "I'm such an alert, clever, creative, intelligent, productive person that being out of the work world wouldn't suit me." There is a strong implication that anyone who can stand staying home is inferior.

Almost all the child raisers we interviewed agreed (many emphatically) that going bananas was a real problem. *But all went on to describe their personal solutions to the problem.* All agreed that if child raising was a priority, the problem could be solved in many ways without returning to work outside the home. The child-raiser–housewife role, like any other job, has boring parts and interesting parts. Mothers agree that the child-raising part is more exciting than the housekeeping part. "Decide on practical priorities," says Cathy McAllister, "—children first, housework last."

Some mothers feel that if they are at home the house must pass the white-glove test. Windows must sparkle and furniture must shine. And they worry that if they don't serve gourmet meals someone will say, "Aha, I knew she watched TV all day!"

Where it is practical and affordable, mothers should take advantage of help with the house. Staying home is not a sin that must be atoned for by slaving three hours a day over a hot stove. There is no reason for a mother to feel guilty about using a diaper service, a cleaner, or any other aid that will free her for her most important job—that of being a child raiser. Nor should she feel guilty about letting her housekeeping standards slip for a while. Focusing on the interesting part of the child-raiser–housewife role is not only beneficial for the child, it makes Mom's job more interesting too.

This is not to say that mothers don't sometimes feel that child raising has its boring times. Get a group of mothers together, and sooner or later someone will say, "Well, did you ever have a stimulating conversation with a two-year-old?"

As teachers, we have had *many* interesting conversations with young children. Once a mother thinks of herself as a teacher, her job will not be so boring. Mothers often think of teaching as limited to academic skills, and then think they might as well leave it to *Sesame Street*. But teaching is much more than that. If a mother tries to seriously answer her two-, three-, or four-year-old's questions, she will find herself doing research, and learning more than she ever learned since she left school. It's a truism that to explain something simply and accurately you must understand it well. And a very young child's questions can lead to an exploration of physics, biology, astronomy, meteorology, chemistry, etc. "Why does it get dark at night?" "Why is the glass one breakable but the plastic one isn't?" "Why would you get my cold if you finished the milk in my cup?" A mother who enjoys learning new things will be helping her child explore the world, and preventing boredom with her own role at the same time, if she answers such questions seriously.

Parents can also try to include children in activities that interest them. Not all activities need to be specifically child-oriented. A mother we know used to bring her daughter on weekly botany walks. As the group clustered around a specimen with plant keys and magnifying glasses, trying to determine the species, the little girl announced, "I know! It a flower!" Her daughter enjoyed the trips very much—on her own level.

Ruth Cohen finds, "Going bananas is a real problem for people if they haven't developed themselves as persons." Boredom is probably worst for women who have few interests of their own. Both men and women often let their work be the focus of their life, which is one reason so many people have difficulty adjusting to retirement. The mother who is at home is often tempted to blame her boredom on the child and look for the outside stimulation of a job. Yet this need could be met in a different and perhaps ultimately more satisfying way, by developing interests in new areas.

Most mothers agree that getting out of the house and doing *something*, every day if possible, is very important. This is sometimes easier said than done. The time a mother feels most down in the dumps is the time she finds it hardest to mobilize herself to go out and be active.

A few mothers we interviewed admitted they *had* occasionally "gone bananas," yelled at their children, or broken down and cried. "When everything gets too much, I cry. Then I willfully push myself to do something—like make arrangements for an evening out. Activity seems to be the answer."

Many mothers feel guilty about expressing a need for time off, and feel they can justify getting a sitter or asking Dad to watch the baby only if they are working or taking a class. Lawyers, mechanics, and engineers don't feel guilty about needing to have some time off to relax. Mothering is no different.

Child raising is a job, and like any other job no one can stand to do it twenty-four hours a day, seven days a week. It will not harm a baby to be left with a reliable sitter once or twice a week while Mom and Dad go to a movie—but there is a way it can harm the mother's state of mind if she doesn't go out!

A class or a *very* part-time job can be a real relief. Just stepping outside the child-raiser–housewife role a few hours a week can make a huge difference. "To work or not to work" need not be the question. Michael Ellis watches the children one evening a week while his wife, Claudia, teaches a college adult education class in natural-foods cookery. Claudia always wanted to have a family and she is happy as a mother, but once a week she enjoys the opportunity to teach, meet new people, earn some money, and get a break from being with the children. Whether a mother is taking a class to keep in touch with her field, preparing for work she hopes to begin when the children are older, or simply going to a dance class for exercise and fun, it's wonderful to have that break.

For classes to take, check the local college. High-school districts, too, often offer adult education classes. City park and recreation departments have classes in everything from batik to car repair. Science museums offer courses. Synagogues and churches have discussion groups. For mothers with interests in a special area, there are organizations that offer classes, many of which are free. The Audubon Society can help budding bird watchers, and there are clubs for chess players, cyclists, and photographers. Of course, there are also private teachers and schools offering lessons of all kinds. Since aerobic exercise and dance classes are especially popular, these classes often offer free child care to participants.

Mothers who have a skill they would enjoy teaching can advertise in a local paper, or get in touch with the park and recreation department. These departments usually have fewer requirements about diplomas and credentials than high-school or community-college districts. Public schools are sometimes interested in having someone come in after school to teach art, music, and other extracurricular subjects. The local PTA can give advice about this. After-school care centers are sometimes interested in a person who can offer a class to their children, whose parents are at work and cannot drive them to ballet, piano, and so on. Even one half-hour class a week can give a mother a real lift and help drive away the boredom blues.

"I'm Not Cut Out for This"

Being a full-time child raiser can be a rewarding and satisfying job. "I really enjoy being my own boss and staying home. It's fun most of the time. Also, instead of being with other children all day long, I can be with and teach my own," says Cathy McAllister, who decided to leave her elementary-school teaching position in order to spend time with her daughter, who is now three and a half.

But not all mothers find it smooth sailing. And when the going gets rough, say upon entering "the terrible twos," many mothers start wondering if it takes a special kind of person to be a patient, loving parent with this totally uncooperative, rebellious two-year-old.

Of course, it is only natural for child raisers to have doubts during a rocky period when they are forced to raise their voice and scold an uncooperative child. But because of contemporary pressures, this feeling of being inadequate or unsuited sometimes leads to the decision to abdicate the child-raiser role and return to work. It is important for child raisers to realize that rocky periods or unpleasant incidents are virtually universal to the child-raising experience.

It simply is not true that there are "born parent" types who know what to do and do everything right from the beginning. Child raising is a learning experience; no formulas or rules will do. There are only guidelines, to be modified according to the particular situation and a parent's own good sense. The truth is that good parents are made, not born.

Mush Brain

In the first weeks after a new baby arrives, mothers often find themselves leaving the original in the copying machine and forgetting to put money in the parking meter. "This is it," they think. "I've heard of women's brains turning to mush, and now it's happening to me."

It is understandable for a mother who has chosen the child-raiser role to have a certain sensitivity when the subject of intelligence and perceptiveness comes up. Despite the increasing number of women entering the professional and white-collar occupations, the well-ingrained prejudice against women's intelligence has not yet evaporated.

"Maybe you are smart—*if* you have proved it." There is little doubt that one powerful motivating force in the current women's movement is the attempt to disprove by achievements in the work world the notion that females have fluff in their heads. Unfortunately, this may make women child raisers feel that they are inferior. Surprisingly, these feelings can surface even when a mother was well established in the workplace prior to her child-raiser role and is assured of a satisfactory position upon reentry.

Of course, there is no research to support the idea that women have an inferior intelligence to men. There may be some evidence that in certain specific tasks, such as mechanical ability, women may be slightly less capable. But this is a very small difference, if any, and is a statistical average. An individual woman can have a mechanical ability far above average for both sexes, and it would be a gross distortion of this data to propose that girls should not be taught mathematics and mechanical engineering. Women have the same average intelligence as men.

Unfortunately, attitudes lag far behind current research, and feelings of inferiority are common. "I need intellectual stimulation," complained one full-time mother in a mothers' group. Another suggested she use the baby's nap time to read. The mother rejected that idea and asked if anyone would be interested in a book-discussion group. Reading, learning a foreign language by listening to tapes, or any other home activity would not do. The need was not so much for intellectual stimulation as for someone to recognize that she *had* an intellect.

It is natural for mothers who have just met to talk about their children. It is the obvious thing that they have in common. But mothers themselves often assume that is all the other mother is able to talk about. Child raising does not invalidate anyone's opinions about politics, music, or philosophy, or diminish her abilities. The mother discussing children's shoe stores on the park bench may just have had some photographs published or been a guest soloist with the local symphony orchestra, if anyone thought to ask her.

What Do You Do, Mommy?

Shannon Dooley's mother was an elementary-school teacher in Georgia. She had decided to be a full-time mother and had given up teaching before her first child was born. She felt sure she was doing the best thing for Shannon and her sister.

When Shannon turned three she started going to a morning preschool program in a preschool–day care center. One day the crushing blow fell. Shannon came home and said, "Today we talked about what all the mommies do. Christine's mommy works in the grocery store. David's mommy's a nurse. I told them you cook supper."

Mothers who have given up work they enjoy for their children's sake are understandably upset by such scenes. Instead of appreciating her sacrifice, some children have the idea that their mother is somehow an embarrassment. The older the child, the worse the embarrassment can be. Shannon's older sister, a sophisticated young lady already going to kindergarten, carefully hid what she saw as her mother's shortcomings. "She's a teacher, she just isn't teaching right now."

Hard as it is at the time, mothers who plan to go to work when their children get older can take comfort in knowing that their children will see things differently in a few years. The three-year-old who is embarrassed about having a mother who does not hold a paying job will feel quite comfortable later saying, as one second-grader the authors spoke to did, "My mother didn't work when I was little, but she does now." Older children find it quite reasonable to think that their mother spent extra time with them when they were small, and if they have the role model of a working mother in their later years, there is no reason why their career choices or goals should be influenced.

Some mothers find it helpful to explain to children (at a level appropriate to the child's age) what they do. Even children of seven or eight often have little idea of what goes into running a household, or what activities their mothers are involved in. An eight-year-old, asked what her mother did while she was in school, replied, "I don't know. I guess she just watches TV."

There is a strong cultural idea that leisure must be earned by hard work. Some mothers feel guiltily that perhaps they do not work as hard as wage earners, and overcompensate by not taking enough breaks for themselves. A mother who has seen through the prejudices about "nonworking" mothers can feel comfortable knowing that she does indeed work even if she does not hold a paying job, and can explain this to her child. And there is no need for a mother to feel embarrassed about taking a break or hide from her child that a friend dropped by and she actually sat down for a cup of coffee. As Maria Martinelli says, "Sometimes I *do* have a doughnut and I *do* watch TV. I figure I earn my breaks as surely as the women who work outside the home. All workers deserve rest."

Am I Wasting My Talents?

Anita Little sat on a park bench watching her toddler play. "I taught kindergarten for a number of years," she said. "Each year the parents got to request which teacher they wanted their child to have. The year I left, sixty parents had chosen my class." She looked at her son. "Sometimes I wonder..." She let the sentence drift.

Nurses, teachers, social workers, and others in the helping professions seem to find it especially difficult to spend all their time helping one little person grow for five years when they could be helping hundreds of people. The nursing shortage, or the knowledge that a hiring freeze in the agency means fewer clients will be served, weighs on the mind of the mother at home. The fact that these professions all require years of preparation make not using the hard-won skill even more difficult.

Child raisers who are professionals often regret not using their skill as well as feeling low self-esteem in the absence of peer praise and recognition. These are not imaginary concerns, and any career woman will need to confront these issues before beginning full-time child raising. If they are not resolved, these doubts can diminish what could have been a very satisfying experience.

Most of the career women we interviewed who worked before and after a period of full-time child raising agreed that by doing both they were fulfilling equally strong needs. There was a consensus that ideally it would not be a choice. But women who felt the superwoman role was unworkable recognized that the price of fulfilling themselves as mothers was an interruption in their career or work life. In the long run, having done both can be a good feeling. "I took six years off to stay home with Eddy," said Elizabeth Jacobs, a publicist for a large New York agency. "I'm back at work now, and I love it, but I'll never regret those years at home with him. They were good years for both of us."

Don't Be a Block Mother Unless You Want to Be

Some mothers enjoy having their house be the one all the kids flock to after school. They like dishing out cookies and advice, being the first to hear about the joys and providing a shoulder for the woes. But there are other mothers, like Rosa Martinez, who feel taken advantage of. Every mother on the block has put her down as the person to call if a child is suddenly taken ill at school. The teachers assume she will always be available to drive on field trips, make costumes for the school play, and coordinate the fund-raising bake sale. Rosa feels she is doing double and triple duty because other mothers are not pulling their own weight.

It helps for a mother at home to remember that she *is* a working mother. Being busy is a perfectly valid reason for not taking on extras, whether one is busy with earning money or with family projects. As we discussed earlier, taking part in some activities outside the home can really help the tendency to feel lonely and isolated. But every mother should *choose* to get involved in 4H, Brownies, the PTA, or other projects—and not allow anyone to railroad her.

Is Mothering Being Overprotective?

Women who are considering leaving full-time employment in order to spend more time with their baby or child often wonder whether the added attention will spoil the child, and mothers who are child raisers are often at a loss for words when accused of being overconcerned or overprotective because they have rejected the full-time day care option. This is a sensitive issue for many of the full-time child raisers we interviewed; many feel that love and attention and protectiveness are all beneficial to their children, yet they are concerned about being overprotective, too. Most are aware that a neurotic, overprotective mother could harm a child's emotional development.

Perhaps the best way to look at this question is that mothers cannot love a child too much, as long as that love does not interfere with recognition of and respect for the child's need to grow and develop and become increasingly independent.

There is no evidence that strong emotional ties with the mother in the early years will produce a weak and dependent character later in life. On the contrary, child-development experts generally agree that a close bond is conducive to the development of a strong, secure personality. This issue did not worry Sally Brown, a telephone repair technician for Southern Bell, who took an extended leave from her job to raise her two children. When asked if she thought too much love might be harmful to a child, she replied, "I spoiled my kids lots, and I'm proud of it. If that's what they mean by spoiling," she added, "I don't think you can do too much of it."

Financial Pressures

In the spread-out newspapers on the floor under the easel, a help-wanted ad catches a mother's eye. "Twelve thousand dollars a year," she thinks dreamily. "What I could do with a thousand dollars a month..."

Any mother who has second thoughts about the child-raising role versus the financial incentive of full-time work owes it to herself and her family to do some figuring and paperwork. The net monetary gain may be small. Full-time care in a day care center averages about $100 a week for infants and $50 a week for preschoolers, according to the Day Care Council of America. Family day care homes cost about $40 a week, and a sitter is about $130 a week at minimum wage for a forty-hour week. In addition, that $1,000-a-month income is *not* the take-home pay. There are commute costs and work clothes. Perhaps some lunches out. What would added income do to the tax bite? Would a job mean using more convenience foods or hiring someone to paint that room or recover that sofa? Some mothers are surprised to find how little they would actually net per hour.

Of course, if a woman will be earning, say, $2 an hour net, after deducting work-related expenses, and that $80 a week is necessary to pay the bills, she may decide to work. But a part-time job or work at home may be economical as well as beneficial for the children. Unfortunately, single parents frequently find themselves in a no-choice situation and cannot work it out to be a full-time or even part-time child raiser. However, working mothers pay a price. Worry over their child's welfare is a leading cause of stress in working mothers of young children, and the destructive effects of full-time work combined with parental responsibilities are well documented.

Sometimes there is a concern at having no separate funds, even though the family income may be adequate. A woman who has always worked may be uncomfortable asking her husband for spending money. A young Chicago waitress felt frustrated. "When I worked I always bought him a nice birthday present. This year was the first time I wasn't working. I didn't know what to do. Finally I asked him for some money to buy fabric and I sewed him a shirt."

Another mother spoke bitterly of not having the money to hire a sitter so she could take a class and get a break from her five-month-old baby once a week. "Can't you save it out of grocery money?" a friend asked. *"He's* got his heart set on a new car," she replied. "If I managed to feed the family on *five dollars a week*, every penny I saved would be used for the new car. I think I'll get a job." This kind of restriction can be wearing on the mother and strain relationships with the husband and the child. A clear understanding based on a frank and open discussion of the budget and how it provides for the mother's financial needs is very helpful.

Reentry

Since most mothers plan to work at some time in their lives, reentry is a major concern. At present, in the United States adequate child care leaves are generally unavailable. In addition, the existing work options and job arrangements are very limited, so that the majority of workers do not have the choice of returning to their job on a part-time basis or bringing their work home. Most workers who leave their jobs in order to be full-time child raisers will have to find new jobs when they reenter the work world. (However, as we will discuss in Part Three, this is beginning to change.)

Mothers reentering the job market find it easiest to get work in traditional women's fields. Clerical and secretarial skills are relatively easy to brush up. Changes in the way offices are run are not major, and it is possible to learn to use a word processor before starting the job search. Reentering career-track positions is more of a problem, and health careers are more difficult to start again because changes in these fields are so rapid.

It is important for women who plan to return to work to keep their professional licenses current. Nurses, CPAs, dental assistants, real-estate brokers, and many others are required to take classes. If a mother lets her license lapse during child-raising years, she may find the requirements for getting the license have been upgraded and she is no longer eligible.

Career counselors note that many women who have been away from work for a period of years think of going into a new field when they do return to work. If a child raiser has some idea of what field she may later go into, it is a good idea to take classes or do volunteer work in that area. For the mother who is not sure, counselors often recommend a class in computers because this technology is affecting so many fields.

When the time comes to look for employment, many colleges have career offices with counselors who specialize in helping reentering women. There are also a number of nonprofit agencies across the country that have funding to help with this situation. Employers report they are usually very pleased with reentering women as employees; they find such women are typically mature and responsible. The National Commission on Working Women reports that older women have better attendance records than younger employees and one sixth the rate of job turnover of women in their twenties.

Men, unfortunately, have a difficult time explaining even a six-month gap in their résumé. Many employers still have the idea that a man who would take time off to be with his children lacks motivation and a serious commitment to his career. Some men try to cover the gap by hiding the fact that they were staying home with their children. A prospective employer is told they were freelancing or writing a book. Other men turn to self-employment and never reenter the job market as an employee. A very few men find employers who simply hire them on the basis of their qualifications and accept the fact that they took time off. It is to be hoped that the number of such enlightened employers will increase, so that men can have the option of experiencing full-time fatherhood.

PART THREE

The Family Here and Abroad

Chapter Eleven

Solutions in Other Countries: Help for Child Raisers and Working Parents

The Solution: More Choices

Many European countries offer working and nonworking parents more choices in handling their child-raising responsibilities than are currently available in the United States. We can learn much from ongoing programs in Europe, and these can serve as models or be adapted for pilot programs in this country. The day care advocates' claim "Women have no choice, we need more full-time day care" is simplistic and narrow-minded in a world where other industrialized countries, in many ways similar to our own, provide viable alternatives for working fathers and mothers who wish to avoid full-time day care for their children in the earliest months or years.

Despite "motherhood and apple pie," the prevailing attitude in the United States is that the family and its needs "should be seen and not heard"; that is, the life of the family can proceed as long as it does not in any way interfere with the work world and the demands of a fulltime job. In many European countries the attitude is quite different. Family life and the work world are seen as equally essential and mutually complementary elements of the society, and therefore the prevailing attitude is that the government and private industry must be sensitive to and make concessions for the ever-present needs of working parents and their children. This is why many concessions are made to pregnant employees and mothers who hold jobs outside their homes. Women are valued both as workers who are making a material contribution to the society *and* as child raisers who play a central role in the continuity of family life in the culture.

Demographics, as well as cultural attitudes, have influenced European labor laws. Countries with a lower than optimal population had to find a way to encourage women to enter the work force to fill jobs, but childbearing had to be made attractive enough to these women workers that reasonable population growth could also be assured. Labor-law changes were instituted after World War I, when the birthrate in some European countries dropped sharply. France, Germany, Sweden, and other countries tried making raising families more attractive through incentives like maternity leaves and family allowances. By the 1920s most European countries offered women workers a paid maternity leave and a guarantee their job would be held for at least six weeks after the birth of a baby. In the sixties and seventies maternity leaves were extended and benefits were improved, with paid child care leaves ranging up to three years. Today the lot of European parents who want to combine family and job responsibilities, simultaneously or in sequence, is far superior to the situation for American parents.

In the United States most employers expect parents to act exactly the same as childless employees, and industry has strongly resisted "government interference" whenever the issues of child care leave and parental sick leave are raised. These expectations are a holdover from a time when few women worked and most fathers had a wife who stayed home full time to care for the children. Although the role of fathers is changing, most employers expect fathers to go about their business free of child care concerns. It is still, for the most part, unacceptable for a man, even a single father, to leave work early to pick up a sick child from school or go to a parent-teacher conference.

As women succeeded in breaking into fields where men had predominated, they became victims of the same traditional expectations. In the U.S. it is understood that in accepting a job a mother is declaring she can do the job as well as a man or a childless woman, and that the employer will not give her any concessions or special consideration because of her dual responsibilities. Women who have careers complain it is even worse for them than for women who have "pink collar" jobs. The women who have worked their way up to the higher levels of management, where they may be the sole woman employed in that capacity, are under the greatest pressure. Having entered the man's world, they are now expected to behave like a man. Such career women worry that they risk not only their own position but the future of other women in the firm if they take off work for a child's illness or refuse to work overtime or on weekends.

Some employers in the United States have raised the equality issue, arguing it would be unfair to offer special privileges to mothers. Of course, rather than expect mothers to perform on the job as men have in the past, it would be possible to make men and women equal by offering mothers and fathers equal opportunity for leave of absence after the birth of a child and parental sick leave. This is exactly what Sweden has done, and other countries are considering following suit.

The creation of real choices by the government and the private sector is an essential ingredient in the solution to the problems of the American working parent. At present, American parents who do not have the financial freedom to be full-time child raisers frequently must choose arrangements that shortchange the material needs of their family or their child's physical and emotional needs, or both. Paid or partially paid maternal and paternal child care leaves, and paid sick-child leaves, like those available in many European countries, would be a big step toward meeting simultaneously the physical, emotional, and material needs of the American family.

Child Care and the Welfare State

Paradoxically, government-supported programs and benefits that help European parents avoid putting their infants and toddlers in someone else's care are often seen as distasteful and reprehensible by Americans because such programs, while helping to preserve the "American values" of a strong commitment to family life, are seen as public welfare. A majority of the Americans who are classified by income as poverty-level are employed, but the words *welfare, social programs,* and *aid to the poor* do not have a positive connotation in the current political climate. Such things as "the welfare fraud" are largely illusory demons, but in a tight and highly competitive economic setting, the social-parasite issue, which raises the specter of hard-working people having to support the unemployed and the underemployed, is on the minds of many Americans.

But the Europeans have avoided, to a great extent, the potential workers-versus-the-unemployed-and-the-poor confrontation by making child care benefits available to everyone, regardless of income level or employment-derived earnings. There is no reason, aside from a lack of motivation on the part of the government, why adaptations of the European system could not be set up in the United States. By making the child care option available to all, the issue of privileges being given to certain groups or classes could be eliminated.

When a particular group is eligible for a social program there will always be those who will raise the social-parasite issue. In the United States, the welfare mother has been the object of much criticism by irate taxpayers who feel she is getting a free ride. If *all* mothers were entitled to an allowance if they chose to stay home with their young children, then there would be no reason to criticize those who took advantage of the program.

Countries that consider it the State's responsibility to provide day care for the children of all working parents look at the full-time mother differently. Government day care programs are very expensive to run, especially infant care programs, where there must be a high ratio of adults to babies. Some countries, like the USSR, which originally vigorously promoted day care for infants, have backed off from that position, realizing that home care is cheaper. In Czechoslovakia, the "Russian system" of Monday-to-Friday round-the-clock day care fell into disrepute when damaging psychological effects were discovered, and a partially paid two-year child leave was instituted. If a mother wants and is able to care for an infant at home, it actually saves the State money. Some countries pass along part of the savings and give mothers an incentive to stay home by offering a paid maternity leave.

Day care in the U.S. is expensive, especially infant care, and it is no less expensive when the government picks up the bill. According to U.S. Department of Labor statistics, direct federal funding of child care in the United States in 1979 cost about $2 billion. In addition, there are indirect subsidies in the form of a child-care tax credit and a tax break for child-care facilities. The total spent by federal, state, and local agencies is about $4 billion, and families annually spend about $6 billion out of their own pocket. A large portion of annual government expenditures has gone to low-income families through such programs as Title XX of the Social Security Act, providing assistance to pay for child care costs, and also funds to upgrade the quality of day care facilities. Yet, even with $600 million going to Title XX in the 1980 fiscal year, all of the combined federal programs did not come close to achieving their modest goal of providing day care for low-income families. Now much of the cost of child care has been shifted to state governments, but the high cost remains the same.

The American perspective on social programs is constantly changing. When the Social Security Act was passed in 1935 many people vigorously opposed it as the first step toward socialism. Now Social Security is well established, and conservatives and liberals alike support the program. A child care leave insurance plan could be a federal government program that parents and parents-to-be would pay into on a voluntary basis, the same way that self-employed people in California can voluntarily pay into a state disability-insurance program. As with the California state disability program, there could be a minimum number of months of participation in the plan required before a parent could draw benefits, and enrollees would have to sign up for the plan for a minimum number of years. Like retirement benefits paid through Social Security, both payments and benefits would be proportional to income. Of course, child care leave insurance should be designed so that either parent could pay into the plan and stay home and draw benefits after a baby's arrival.

Before legislators jump on the bandwagon, allocating greater and greater funds in an attempt to carpet the country with day care facilities, it would be helpful for them to analyze exactly what they are trying to accomplish, and if they have the time and the persuasion, it would be useful to look across the Atlantic with a large telescope and examine what solutions European countries have already developed. If we assume that the current trend of full-time employment for both fathers and mothers is going to continue, then the appropriate question is, what kind of choices can we offer these parents so that they can fulfill their responsibilities both as breadwinners and as child raisers? Full-time day care, no matter how heavily funded, is not an answer, because it comes from looking at only half the problem.

Before legislation and programs can be created that truly give parents choices in meeting their financial and child-raising responsibilities, the government must overcome a very one-sided perspective on the problem. A recent government report on day care summarized the problems of the working mother and her family without once mentioning the subject of emotional needs of children or the possibility of a working mother wanting to spend more time with her child. Of course, the possibility that early separation from parents for forty or fifty hours a week might have a harmful effect on children was not even hinted at. These omissions say a great deal about the Administration's perspective on the problem, and it is vital that this change so that the dual responsibilities of the working parent be recognized, as they are in many European countries.

Just as parents have a responsibility to meet their children's psychological *and* material needs, the government should concern itself both with the need for productivity and employment and with the emotional needs of family life. With $10 billion a year being spent for child care, and subsidized nonprofit day care programs spending as much as $1,000 a month per family, it is reasonable and realistic to create optional paid or reduced-pay parental child care leaves and parental sick-child leaves for all working parents.

Help for Full-Time Child Raisers

Women in the United States who decide to take an extended leave in order to be full-time child raisers face the dual pressures of loss of income and uncertainty of reentry. In many European countries these problems have been solved to a great extent by giving a mother's allowance and by passage of laws guaranteeing that a woman will get her position or a "suitable alternative" back with no loss of seniority after a leave of absence.

In some countries the employer pays the child care leave benefits and is later fully or partially reimbursed by social security programs, and in others the State picks up the tab directly. Government policy determines the length of the child care leave and what percentage of the salary or what fixed benefit amount a mother will receive. Unlike the United States, where only a few prestigious jobs offer maternity leaves of up to six months, in these countries all working women receive equal coverage in the length of their child care leave.

As the table shows, Spain and Hungary allow a mother to stay

Comparison of Child Care Leaves Available in Some Industrialized Countries

Country	Length of Leave with Job Guarantee[a]	Length of Paid Child Care Leave and Benefit Amount
Austria	1 year	1 year, fixed monthly benefit[b]
Czechoslovakia	2 years	6 months, 90% of salary
Denmark	5 months	5 months, 50% of salary *or* 2 months, 100% of salary
France	2 years[c]	2½ to 4½ months, 90% to 100% of salary
Hungary	3 years	6 months, 100% of salary 2½ years, fixed benefit amount
Italy	1 year	3 months, 100% of salary 6 months, 30% of salary
Spain	3 years	2 to 3½ months, 75% of salary
Sweden	1 year	6 months, 90% of salary 3 months, fixed benefit amount 3 months, lower fixed benefit amount
United Kingdom	6 months[d]	1½ months, 90% of salary 4½ months, fixed benefit amount
U.S.	1½ months[e]	1½ months, fixed benefit amount
USSR	1 year	2 months, fixed benefit amount
West Germany	6 months	2 months, 100% of salary 4 months, fixed benefit amount

[a] These figures do not always apply to self-employed working parents.

[b] Benefit is higher for single parent.

[c] A two-year leave is available to employees of companies with over 100 employees. Employees of smaller firms are eligible for a one-year leave.

[d] A woman must have completed two years of service and must work up to eleven weeks before her due date.

[e] This figure is included for comparison. There is generally no child care leave available in the U.S. This figure represents the typical maternal disability leave, which sometimes may function as a very short child care leave.

home for three years before she must return to work. Spain has an additional excellent provision that permits a parent to work half time until a child is six. It is the only country that takes into account the needs of three- to six-year-old children. However, even programs that allow a new mother to stay home for six months or a year are a big improvement over the typical situation in the U.S.

While all the countries in the table except the United States offer child care leaves, only Italy, France, Spain, and Sweden have given equal opportunity to fathers. In these countries, after the initial weeks, either parent may take advantage of a leave of absence following the birth of a child. Belgium and the Netherlands are currently considering adopting such a policy.

The Swedish policy, which is aimed at giving men and women equal opportunity to work outside the home and to be child raisers, is particularly flexible. Either parent may take a six-month leave after the birth of a child, and an additional six months may be taken anytime until the child is eight years old. The hours of these additional 180 days may be divided up, allowing a parent to work part time until the child reaches school age.

Dr. Gregor Katz, a child psychiatrist in Stockholm, feels the child care leave policy is very beneficial for Swedish families, but notes that "most mothers would like even longer if it were available." Eva Wadell, an elementary-school teacher in Stockholm who now takes her fourteen-month-old son, Carl Johan, to a day care home, emphatically agrees that while she is grateful to have been able to stay home with her baby for six months, she would gladly have taken a longer leave. Eva returned to her teaching job six months after Carl Johan was born, and then her husband, Jan, thirty-four, a middle-school teacher, stayed home for a three-month paid extension. Jan, who says he wanted to have close contact with his child at an early age, is in the forefront of a new movement toward greater involvement of fathers in child raising. In 1979 about 10 percent of fathers in Sweden took some time off during an initial six-month leave; the average leave taken was a little over one month. About one third of fathers used some time out of the additional six-month special allowance to stay home with their children. "While the program is available to men, most men don't use it still," explains Eva. "But it is gradually changing and becoming more and more common."

After the initial months in which parents taking a child care leave receive full or 90 percent salary, additional leave time is poorly paid or unpaid. Austria and West Germany offer a subsistence-level allowance, and other countries offer even less, looking at the benefit as a supplement to family income. However, there are no restrictions on other income, as there are with U.S. welfare programs like Aid to Families with Dependent Children. If a mother chooses to supplement the allowance by doing some work at home, her child raiser's benefits are not reduced. Of course, she also has the right to return to her job at any time, and in some countries like the USSR she has the right to return to work on a part-time basis anytime within the child care leave.

In Europe, most mothers choose to take advantage of a paid leave of absence and do not return to work until that leave has run out. Interviews indicate that many mothers in this country would enthusiastically welcome the opportunity to stay home, even at a reduced salary, if they could have a guarantee of getting their job back with no loss of seniority or benefits.

In addition to child care leaves, European countries have other arrangements that help parents who want to be child raisers. In many European countries, as well as in the United States, there is a high divorce rate. Single parents in Europe, too, often find they must seek employment if they are not granted adequate alimony and child support. However, divorced parents in France and Sweden benefit from a system of child-support payments that guarantees their check will arrive every month. The U.S. Census Bureau found that half of all child-support payments are partial or delinquent. These payments can make the difference between having to work a full-time job and being able to work part time and spend some time at home with children.

In Sweden, when a couple divorces, the parent who does not have custody of the child must pay a maintenance allowance. (About 10 percent of single parents are men.) This allowance may be agreed upon by the couple themselves, or may be mandated by the court. If the parent who is supposed to pay the allowance cannot or does not pay, the parent who has custody is paid a maintenance advance by the government. The French have a similar system, whereby the government will pick up on child-support payments if the parent who is obligated to pay them defaults. Knowing that child-support money will arrive regularly allows divorced parents to plan their budget, and helps single parents who want to work part time.

Help for Working Parents

In Europe, the understanding that parents who are employed have dual responsibilities has led to the enactment of many special laws. In a number of countries protection starts during pregnancy, with regulations forbidding an employer to ask a pregnant woman to work overtime, night shifts, Sundays, or holidays. After the birth, if a mother returns to work, some countries continue to give special consideration to her. In the USSR nursing mothers and mothers with children under a year old can transfer to less strenuous work at the same pay as their regular job. They cannot be required to work overtime or to be sent out of town on business until the youngest child is eight years old.

Mothers are given *paid* time off to nurse or feed their infant in Italy, France, the USSR, and other countries. This is in sharp contrast to the U.S., where women in a number of fields have been barred from nursing their infants on their own coffee and lunch breaks. In Iowa City a firefighter lost her job and had to go to court to establish her right to nurse her baby on her own time. Other women have had to resort to such extremes as having a sitter bring their baby to a gas-station restroom near the place of work, because the employer barred the baby from the premises. Nursing-time allowance varies from country to country, ranging from one to two hours a day, and lasts until the baby is nine months old in Spain, a year old in Italy and France, and as long as necessary in West Germany. This time is paid time, given in addition to regular breaks. Some larger businesses with many women employees have a nursing room at the place of business, so sitters or relatives caring for a new baby can bring the child to the place of work. Other mothers find it more convenient to add one hour of their nursing break onto their lunch hour and then go home one hour early. In Italy, either parent may take this time off. If the father is widowed or the baby is in the father's custody after a divorce, the father is entitled to take the two extra paid hours a day to spend time with his child. Some parents who are sharing their baby's care alternate days, with the father going home early one day and the mother the next.

Paid or unpaid parental sick leave is another aid to the working mother, and in some countries the father may share parental sick leave. In the United States most employees are not provided with parental sick leave, and are put in the unpleasant position of having to lie and claim they are sick themselves or use up vacation days if one of their children is ill. In Sweden, since 1980, parents have been entitled to sixty days per year for each child, until the child is twelve. Either the mother or the father may take this leave, and in practice they do tend to share this responsibility. The Swedish Ministry of Health and Social Affairs reports that on the average fathers are home the same amount of time as mothers. While Sweden has the most liberal policy, other countries do offer parental sick leave on a more limited basis. Even in countries where there is no formal parental sick-leave policy, it is common practice for employers to allow parents to stay home if a child is sick—unless, as one Danish official joked, a child is mysteriously ill every Monday and Friday for a year!

While benefits such as nursing breaks and adequate paid parental sick leaves are no substitute for paid child care leaves, these benefits very nicely complement a system in which a basic child care leave is available. These programs indicate a willingness to help ease the burdens of working parents and show a sympathy and respect for the "invisible" problems of child raising.

France adopted a thirty-nine-hour workweek in 1982, and the government has promised a thirty-five-hour workweek by 1985. In Denmark, Sweden, and other countries, pressure is building to institute a thirty-hour workweek. This would involve a six-hour workday, five days a week. The Institute for Social Research in Denmark collaborated with the Board of Health and National Statistics Bureau in interviewing women to determine what changes were happening in the family pattern. The study showed that most women preferred to work part time if they could afford it. It recommended a reduction of working hours for *both* parents, with compensation for the loss of income as a method of allowing both parents to work while assuring that children would be able to spend time with their parents. If implemented, a six-hour day, combined with a flexitime schedule, would mean that children would have to be cared for by someone other than a parent only half time.

These European systems of benefits to employed and on-leave parents are working, giving child raisers choices and flexibility that U.S. parents don't have. We can learn much from the European experience and adapt it to the needs of American parents, providing real choices for a balanced, sane approach to the dual responsibilities of wage earning and child raising.

Chapter Twelve
Solutions in the United States

New Options for Workers

While the very important option of a paid child care leave is not generally available to the American working parent, other options like job sharing and flexitime are becoming more and more common. The good news is that change, although slow-paced, is happening, and it is likely that this change will accelerate as the government and private industry continue to feel the pressure from a work force that contains a growing constituency of working parents who are concerned with the combined responsibilities of work and raising a family. The first White House Conference on Families in 1980 recognized this problem and urged greater flexibility in work hours and more liberal parental sick-leave policies to enable parents to "hold jobs while maintaining a strong family life." A 1980 Gallup Poll provided confirmation that the majority of American workers would like to have the options of job sharing and flexible working hours. While the U.S. is still far behind many European countries in giving parents basic options they need, these changes in attitudes show that progress is being made.

One alternative to the forty-hour workweek that has opened up in recent years is job sharing. The Department of Labor estimates that about 22 percent of American workers currently work part time, but traditionally most part-time work has been low-status, low-paying employment, and has not offered health coverage, sick leave, pension plans, and other benefits. Job sharing evolved as a way for people to work at permanent part-time jobs in a variety of employment fields, some of which did not have part-time workers in the past.

Although the number of men interested in a job-sharing option is increasing, so far fields that employ mainly women have been most responsive to pressure to introduce this alternative to the forty-hour workweek. Job sharers include teachers, nurses, flight attendants, school bus drivers, and teachers. Some job-sharing partners split their days, with one taking mornings and the other working afternoons. Others split their week; one partner might work Monday and Wednesday, while the other works Tuesdays and Thursdays, with Fridays alternating. A few job sharers even alternate weeks. In all cases, vacation time and fringe benefits are prorated.

The advantages of job sharing to parents who want to spend more time with their children are obvious, but there are advantages to employers as well. Two heads *are* better than one, and job sharers with different specialized training and perspectives can often solve a problem that would have perplexed an individual employee. Also, job sharing can increase productivity, because employees have more energy for the job in the hours that they are at work, and it enables a firm to keep a valued employee who has just had a baby or just begun sharing child care responsibilities, or who is approaching retirement. This cuts down on training and recruitment costs. Because so many people find job sharing a satisfying arrangement, morale is good and job turnover is lowered. Absenteeism is reduced, and when one partner is ill the other can often fill in by working extra hours. This eliminates the confusion of a temporary substitute who does not really know what is going on.

Government agencies see job sharing as a good way to increase the number of women and handicapped employees and have been especially receptive to job sharing. Approximately fifteen states have now passed job-sharing legislation. In February 1978 Governor

Hugh Carey of New York issued an executive order encouraging state agencies to implement alternative work-schedule arrangements. By October 1980, 18 percent of part-time workers were job sharing, and 84 percent of the state agencies had part-time workers. In California two bills were passed in 1981 providing reduced-work-time options. As of April 1982, about four thousand state employees were voluntarily working part time. This represents a 28 percent increase in just one year. Forty-one percent of California's county governments have job sharers, and all but two counties offer some form of permanent part-time employment with benefits. School districts have also been receptive to job sharing. More than 37 percent of California's school districts now have teachers who share a job.

Change has been slower in the private sector. More small firms have implemented job sharing than large corporations, although many large corporations have plans on the drawing board. A recent Harris survey found that 70 percent of the nation's major corporations plan to adopt a job-sharing policy within the next five years.

In economic hard times, employees are often especially hesitant to go to their employer with a suggestion that they share their job. Particularly if there is no obvious reason for the request, like a baby on the way, employers may see the request as a lack of commitment to the job. Employees are concerned that in a tight job market they may be replaced if they appear to show a lack of commitment. It is a great irony that in a time when we have the highest unemployment in decades there are people who want and can afford to reduce their number of hours through job sharing and are not able to do so.

There are agencies across the country that counsel people who are planning to approach their supervisor with a job-sharing proposal or who are looking for a shared job (see Appendix II). And the Association of Part-time Professionals was recently formed to promote part-time professional employment opportunities. Based in Washington, D.C., this organization has begun to organize local chapters, and this area of job sharing and part-time work is opening up.

Flexitime, or overlapping work schedules, is another option that can help parents to minimize the number of hours their children spend in day care. In flexitime there is a core period when all the employees are at the place of work, usually from 10:00 A.M. to 3:00 P.M. Some employees arrive as early as 7:00 A.M. and leave at 3:00 P.M., while others arrive as late as 10:00 and stay until 6:00 P.M. The Department of Labor estimates that about 7.6 million workers are on flexible work schedules.

Companies use flexitime for a number of reasons. It increases productivity by allowing employees who are "morning people" to come in early, while the night owls who can't think straight until 10:00 A.M. can come in at the time they will work their best. Flexitime can also be used to increase the company's productive hours without paying overtime. Some West Coast firms use it because they need people to come in to do business with East Coast firms when they open for work at 8:00 or 9:00 A.M. Eastern time (5:00 or 6:00 A.M. Pacific time). Flexitime can benefit workers and the community by cutting down on rush-hour traffic, reducing commute times, and shortening the total time away from home.

When both parents work full-time flexitime jobs, they have all the stresses associated with combining full-time work and parenting; however, they can increase the number of hours they spend with their children. If one parent starts at 7:00 A.M., the other can get the children ready for school or for day care. The parent who left early can pick the children up shortly after 3:00 P.M. For school-age children, this means a parent is there when they leave for school and when they return. Children below first grade will still benefit from the additional ten to fifteen hours a week spent with their parents.

Other variations of flexitime include gliding time (employees can vary starting time from day to day), variable day (employees can debit and credit hours from day to day), and maxiflex (employees work a set number of hours within a given pay period, with no core time). Some parents use flexible time options to reduce the number of days they work each week. Four ten-hour days is a popular arrangement. If both parents can work a compressed week on different schedules, their children need to be in day care only three days a week. And a staggered maxiflex schedule for both parents can mean that a child would need outside care only twenty hours a week or less. Unfortunately, the disadvantage of this is that the father and mother rarely get to spend time together except on weekends, and that may not be a happy compromise for the parents.

Unions have been critical of flexitime and the compressed workweek. After a long fight for the eight-hour day, they are reluctant to support a return to longer days. However, where the introduction of flexitime includes provisions to ensure employees will not be *forced* to change their work schedules, management and unions have agreed their interests coincide. A two-and-a-half-month flexitime experiment conducted by the Kentucky Department of Personnel in 1977 shows how employees feel about the flexitime option. Eighty-four percent of employees chose to change from their regular work schedule. A survey at the end of the experiment showed over 90 percent of those responding were pleased with flexitime, including more than 80 percent of the employees who had chosen to remain on their regular schedules. In other words, the American worker likes the idea of flexibility and choice.

There are other changes in personnel policy that are a step in the right direction. These changes do not enable parents to avoid day care, but do make it possible for them to spend a little more time with their children.

One of these changes is "cafeteria benefits." This flexible benefit plan enables employees to convert unwanted benefits into benefits they can use. For example, in a family where both parents are employed full time, both may be covered by their own medical plan *and* their spouse's medical plan. Under a flexible benefit program, this duplicate coverage could be converted into other benefits. One option that may be offered is trading the duplicate coverage for extra days off. This option has obvious advantages to working parents who want to spend more time with their children.

The first flexible benefit plan was introduced in 1974. While few companies offer flexible benefits at present, the idea is beginning to take hold and many companies have consultants working on studying the feasibility of introducing such a program.

Another change that affects working parents is an improvement in parental sick leave. A 1980 survey by Catalyst Career and Family Center found that 29 percent of the Fortune 1300 corporations are now providing days off for children's illnesses. As well as taking the pressure off working parents, and making children feel more secure in knowing they will not be left with some stranger from a babysitting agency when they are feeling miserable, parental sick leave has community health benefits. When parents are not forced to send their children to school or day care even when they are sick, the problem of contagion in these group situations is reduced. "I was sending my three-year-old daughter to a morning program in a place that did full-time day care," reported one pregnant mother who worked part-time as a secretary. "In my eighth month I was catching everything and my doctor told me I better take her out and stay home or I'd jeopardize the new baby."

Some universities, like the University of California in Los Angeles, now offer parental sick leave, and many smaller employers have informal arrangements to accommodate parents with a sick child. "I really appreciate my supervisor's understanding," says Irene Thaler, a child raiser who recently started work as a travel agent after being a full-time child raiser for thirteen years. "I'd only been on the job a few months when my oldest son broke his leg. I didn't know what I was going to do, but she said it was fine for me to take time off to pick him up from school and drive him home." Parental sick leave is badly needed by hard-working parents, and the trend toward recognizing and accommodating this need is an important step in the right direction.

New Options for Fathers

Options in work arrangements are opening up for fathers who want to be full-time or part-time child raisers, and, while progress is slow, organizations like the nationwide Equal Rights for Fathers are putting pressure on legislators and private industry to increase the opportunities for working fathers to participate in the care of their children. Since child raising has traditionally been handled by the mother, options allowing working mothers to spend more time with their children have developed more rapidly, and there are arrangements like permanent part-time work and job sharing that, so far, are easiest to find in pink-collar jobs. The recognition of fathers' interest in child raising, and changes in work arrangements to allow fathers to exercise this option, represent an important step in an overall process of social change that will continue to improve the work and family life of two-paycheck families.

Paternity leave is an important innovation that allows fathers to spend more time with their children. Companies such as AT&T and Procter & Gamble are currently offering unpaid paternity leaves that guarantee reinstatement with no loss of seniority, and the Ford Foundation offers a partially paid six-and-a-half-month leave. Overall, about 10 percent of all U.S. corporations offer paternity leaves. Fathers who participate in these programs frequently discover that, to their surprise, they are endowed with a "maternal instinct"; they are often amazed at their own capacity for sensitivity and caring, in sharp contrast to the macho cultural stereotype.

And the experience of being a full-time child raiser and homemaker results in a new respect for this role. "It is really a job, just like at work," comments one surprised father, a twenty-nine-year-old attorney, who took an unpaid leave of absence to care for his three-year-old son. His surprise shows that at least part of the lack of respect for the homemaker–child-raiser role comes from a lack of firsthand experience by the male segment of the society.

Hopefully, the concept of maternal and paternal child care leaves will eventually be replaced by government and private industry's general adoption of *parental* child care leaves that could be shared by mothers and fathers according to the needs and situation of each family. An important trend-setting law passed by the State of California, effective in 1982, allows all state employee parents, fathers or mothers, to take an unpaid parental leave for up to one year, with a guarantee of no loss of seniority or benefits upon return. An important feature of this law is that it specifically gives this option to fathers as well as mothers, thereby overcoming the common "reverse discrimination" of leaves that are available only to mothers.

The growth of paternal or parental child-care leaves has the effect of accelerating involvement of fathers in child raising by helping fathers to overcome an ingrained reluctance in taking that role. Fathers who would not feel comfortable asking their employer for a child care leave will often take one if it is offered as a matter of company or government policy. Thus, the option of paternity leaves snowballs. The more it is available, the more fathers will take this option, and then the demand will grow for this to be instituted at other companies. But this process needs the support of employers and legislators so fathers can feel that paternal child raising is sanctioned, and that they won't face criticism from their peers. "Most fathers feel they have to be a John Wayne, even though they may secretly care for their child, changing diapers and so on," comments Marvin Philo, co-chairperson of the Sacramento Chapter of Equal Rights for Fathers. "Many of these fathers actively care for their children but don't admit this to anyone."

Besides paternity leave, other work options such as cafeteria benefits, flexitime, and parental sick leave tend to benefit working fathers as well as working mothers, and allow both parents to share work and child raising. Undoubtedly, fathers will continue to play an increasingly important role in their children's daily life, and this can only be beneficial to the children and the family.

While options currently available in the workplace lag far behind the choices that exist for working parents in many European countries, parents can expect to see continued improvement as employers respond to the needs of a growing number of two-career families. Some of the current possibilities, like most short paid child care leaves, are little more than a token in terms of a long-term commitment to child raising. Yet, despite these limitations, many parents have found ways to carve out a child-raiser role for themselves simultaneously utilizing existing options "within the system" and their own adaptability in changing jobs, work schedules, and even life styles. These personal solutions are viable alternatives to full-time day care, operable here and now in our fast-changing society.

Chapter Thirteen

Personal Solutions

While being a full-time child raiser is the first choice for the child's early years, contemporary work and financial pressures frequently require parents to make a compromise with some kind of juggling of child-raising and work responsibilities. In the absence of paid or even unpaid child care leaves, many highly motivated parents have managed to do some fancy footwork and have avoided or substantially postponed putting their children in day care. Using strategies such as part-time work, job sharing, compressed workweeks, self-employment, and work at home, they have created schedules that allow them to spend a lot of time with their children, while still continuing to make a significant contribution to the family income.

Accomplishing this goal often requires innovation in work arrangements and changes in traditional roles and child-rearing practices. Mothers and fathers are sharing parenting responsibilities, and working evenings or weekends, if they must, in order to be sure their child's emotional needs will be met. Currently, one father in ten cares for his children while his wife works full time, and one father in four is home with his children while his wife works at part-time employment. However, in families where avoiding day care is a priority, a much higher percentage of fathers actively share in child care.

A surprisingly large number of mothers care for their children while they work. Almost one out of every five mothers who works part-time and one out of ten full-time working mothers are working while caring for their child. This arrangement is only one of many possible solutions.

The authors interviewed working parents who used a number of different strategies to avoid placing their child in day care: job sharing, taking a child to work, self-employment, and work at home. Even some single parents, despite typical shortages of time, energy, and money in their unique situation, have found ways to avoid putting their children in full-time day care. These parents come from different parts of the country and have different levels of education. But we found that the common denominator is that all these parents value the child-raising experience and believe that the time they spend with their children is very important to their child's emotional development.

The Child at Home

College Professor/College Professor

For the last nine years Patricia and William Freiert have been sharing a position in the classics department of Gustavus Adolphus College in St. Peter, Minnesota. While they were still in graduate school, a newspaper article about a couple sharing a position there attracted them to Gustavus Adolphus. William, who finished his graduate work first, began teaching there full time, and when Patricia joined him two years later they began job sharing.

"We intended to have children," said William. "One of the things that attracted us to Gustavus was that job sharing was a possibility there." After many pregnancy-related problems, the Freierts were advised to consider adoption, so it was with a special joy that they celebrated Michael's birth.

From the start they divided his care, with each parent working half a day. After trying different schedules they settled down into a routine of William working in the mornings and Patricia working in the afternoons, with one hour for the midday transition. Each teaches two or three courses a semester. "We know a couple at Carlton College who bring the baby to class, to be handed over to the other parent in the ten-minute break. We tried that a few times but it didn't work for us," Patricia explained. Although Michael refused a bottle, Patricia had no problems with nursing him on this schedule; she managed quite well by nursing him before she left for class and again upon her return.

Patricia enjoys the combination of teaching and mothering. "I found that in being a new mother some problems in mothering loomed huge. But they seemed minor if I got a few hours away a day. The work and time at home balanced each other. Neither became the focus of my whole life. I wasn't weighed down by a full teaching load, and I had time away from the house every day." William is equally pleased with the arrangement. "I'm sure I'd be much less close if I only saw him [Michael] a few hours in the evening. The nicest thing about academia," he adds, "is that you can adjust your schedule. It's more natural, you can adjust to your own rhythms."

The Freierts continued sharing housework as they had before Michael's birth, though the standards changed somewhat. "We did a lot of playing," said Patricia, "and the housework got kind of chaotic and minimal." At one point when it seemed they just couldn't cope with teaching, the house, and parenting, technology came to the rescue in the form of a dishwasher and a food processor. "I don't know how we'd have managed without a dishwasher!"

When Michael was one and a half, Patricia began sharing child care with a friend. Each mother would take both toddlers one morning a week and have some "sanity time" on another. At three Michael started going to a co-op three mornings a week. Currently the Freierts both are working full time while a colleague takes a leave of absence. Michael now goes to day care twenty-one hours a week, in part because the Freierts feel the opportunity to socialize is especially important to him as an only child and partly so they have more time for class preparation and other class-related work. They still arrange their schedules so the actual hours of teaching do not overlap, making it possible for them to care for Michael when he is sick.

"I wouldn't advise this for the first year of a marriage or a job," cautions Patricia. "We had already shared housework as graduate students, and had already evolved fast, nutritious, cheap meals we like to eat. We had the new job completely in hand before Michael was born. I can't imagine a new job *and* a new child—there are so many little adjustments."

What does Michael think about the arrangement? His parents laugh. "His ideal is to have *both* of us home *all* the time!"

Graphic Artist/Woodworker

"Before we had Vincent there was never any question that we both wanted to work. But we were also very possessive. Neither of us wanted to put him in child care." Yvonne and her husband, Mark Thaler, are both self-employed, so they have flexibility in their schedules. Mark is a craftsman who makes beautiful custom-made hardwood furniture on commission. At the time their son, Vincent, was born, Yvonne, a former Berlitz teacher, was teaching French privately at home. For the first three months of Vincent's life she cut her tutoring to ten hours a week, arranged at times Mark would be home, and then built it back up to twenty hours a week.

"For the first year I was more involved with Vincent," Yvonne explains. "It wasn't fifty-fifty then, more like two-thirds to one-third. I was nursing, so when Mark would put him to sleep he'd cry long and hard. I'd just nurse him to sleep."

A change in the routine came when Yvonne decided that she wanted to try to make money at her painting, which she had been doing as an avocation for several years. She began phasing out of teaching French and into painting, setting up a studio in the basement. Work at home, even with Mark on call, had its problems. "If I heard Vincent crying I wanted to come up, so Mark pushed me to get a studio of my own."

When Vincent was one and a half Yvonne and Mark started on a new strict schedule, working six days a week. On Monday Yvonne would get up early as she wanted, often 5:30 or 6:00 A.M., and go to her studio. She came back at 1:30, and the family would have lunch together. Then Mark would go to work, coming home as late as he wanted, usually 9:00 or 9:30. On Tuesdays, the schedule reversed, with Mark getting up early and Yvonne working into the evening. Whoever was home in the morning took care of lunch preparation, and the afternoon person took care of making dinner. Vincent ate early, and his parents ate a late dinner together at 9:30. The schedule continued with little change, except that Vincent started going to preschool for three hours in the morning, until this year. Now Vincent is in kindergarten from 9:00 A.M. to 3:00 P.M. These extra hours in school mean that neither Yvonne nor Mark has to work late into the evening, and the family can have dinner together.

Sharing Vincent's care has the problems of sharing any job. "What's the right way to bring up Vincent? We have to discuss and work out every problem," says Mark. "But at least we *do* work it out. One person can't say, 'I'm doing all the work so I get to say.' Sharing Vincent's care is the most meaningful thing Yvonne and I do together, and I think I have a better relationship with Yvonne because of it." Yvonne agrees. "We like that we can both talk about him. And Mark knows what it feels like to be stuck at home and also to see all the growing up."

New patterns do not always come easily. Yvonne is proud that she is supporting herself as an artist, but she is surprised at her own ambivalence. "Part of me still wants a strong husband who supports me. On one level I still want the old things. It's an emotional thing, not a rational one." Yvonne also had feelings of jealousy and possessiveness. "In the beginning it was hard for me to even let Mark take care of him." She also recognized an element of competition, which was strongest in the early years. "We both wanted to be special to Vincent. When he fell down we both wondered who he'd run to." Now, with Vincent five, Yvonne and Mark agree, "Vincent is connected to both of us, and we are equally connected to him."

Financial pressures have added some strain. Like many families, Yvonne and Mark have felt the effects of the recession; since neither Yvonne's miniature paintings nor Mark's custom-made furniture is an essential item people will buy even if times are tight, they are in an especially vulnerable position. Being self-employed, there is always the temptation to try to make up the difference by working extra hours. "Sometimes I wish I had more work time," says Mark. "I resent having less time to work than my competitors. Most people doing what I do work fifty or sixty hours a week." Like many artists who put a tremendous amount of labor into a piece, Mark finds that if he really charged for his time he would price himself out of the market. "I have a desk commissioned through a store right now that will sell for $1,750. The store will take $250. I'm supposed to get $15 an hour for my time, but I'll end up getting maybe half that."

As a man, Mark has been aware of some prejudice when he lets people know he is combining work and child raising. "I run into fairly macho people in my line of work. At times I've been embarrassed to say I work part time." A thirty-five-hour workweek is hardly what most people consider part time, but the idea of a man taking *any* hours that could be work hours and using them to spend time with a child is unacceptable to some men.

Both Mark and Yvonne feel that having so much time with his dad will influence Vincent's values, that he won't grow up to join the ranks of the macho. "I'm hoping he'll be more balanced, more compassionate than most men," Mark says.

"Because the society is set up the other way, a man has to decide if it's worth the struggle," says Mark. For Yvonne and Mark, it's been worth it. After five years of both working and sharing Vincent's care, they agree, "It's hard to imagine it being any other way. A different life would seem very strange."

Hairdresser/Maintenance Engineer

Twenty-five-year-old Joanne Manning worked as a hairdresser before her son, Christopher, was born. Four months after his birth she went back to work ten hours a week, leaving Christopher at home with his father, Robert, or with his grandmother. When Christopher was almost two, Joanne became pregnant again and decided to leave her job for a while. Christopher now has a three-month-old sister, Carrie-Anne.

Joanne thought of a way to keep in practice and earn some money at the same time. She set up a beauty salon in her basement, scheduling appointments for the children's nap times or for times Robert is at home. Since Robert, a maintenance engineer at a public school, is now working twelve hours a day, Joanne must schedule appointments for weekends if she wants him to watch the children.

Nap-time appointments are sometimes difficult. Little Carrie-Anne is not on a predictable nap schedule yet, and sometimes Joanne has to excuse herself to calm the baby down before she can continue. But since her business is all by word of mouth, her clients know her situation and are very understanding. Also, by working at home Joanne is able to offer her clients a very reasonable rate. The salon she worked in allowed her a 50 percent commission, so now she can charge just half the beauty-salon price and make the same hourly wage. Under the circumstances, her clients don't mind if the appointment takes a little longer than it otherwise might.

Joanne says she misses the more professional atmosphere of the salon, but she also likes setting her own schedule, and being home for lunch and dinner with the children. "I don't want them to feel pushed off on someone. Now I'm not always running out and leaving them."

Joanne plans to go back to work part-time again when Carrie-Anne gets older. Robert's mother and Joanne's sister have offered to care for the children when she does decide to go back. But for now Joanne is pleased to be able to continue her line of work in her home while taking care of her children.

Social Worker/Public School Principal

Linda Aiello worked for many years as a school social worker. She was part of a child study team that worked to identify, classify, and remediate learning disabilities. She also did family counseling in a private clinic and had some private clients as well.

In her eighth month of pregnancy, Linda left her jobs at the school and the clinic, continuing only with her private clients. When their son arrived, Linda and her husband, Tony, named him Adam.

Linda, thirty-seven, is not planning to have any more children, so it is especially important to her to watch Adam grow up. "I've saved it until now to build up my private practice. My goal is to be with him, and stay with him. As he's able to handle more separation, I'll build it up."

Adam is now six months old, and Linda works seven to ten hours a week, earning about $1,400 a month. She schedules appointments for late afternoons, when Tony, a public-school principal, is home and can care for Adam. When a client must have an early appointment, Linda aims for nap time.

The Aiellos live in a duplex, and when Linda is seeing clients Tony and Adam stay upstairs. Soundproofing is not complete, and when Linda hears that Adam is upset she finds it does take her attention away from the session in progress. Nap times are even more of a problem. Although her clients are very understanding, Linda finds she feels guilty if Adam is awake.

Despite these drawbacks, Linda finds many advantages to working at home. Her office is rent-free, and there's no commute. At the clinic Linda received half of what the client paid; at home she gets the full amount. There are also tax advantages. As renters, the Aiellos do not have the tax deductions they would have if they owned a home. With the business deductions available, Linda can make more with a small private practice at home than working a full-time salaried job.

Combining work and Adam's care is very important to Linda because of her own childhood experiences. "My mother worked full time and I was very resentful. I said I'd never work. But as I grew up I realized work was very important to me. I had to find a compromise."

Linda plans to find a housekeeper as Adam gets older so she can have some additional work time. But time with Adam is very important to her, and she plans to limit herself to fifteen hours a week of counseling.

Weaver

Kay Rudd was fortunate in not having to give up doing work she liked in order to remain with her children. But she was faced with a particularly difficult situation in other respects.

She and her husband adopted two children, one Caucasian and one Vietnamese. When her marriage broke up, Kay was left alone with a one-year-old and a one-and-a-half-year-old.

"At first I couldn't believe it," says Kay. "I kept wanting to say, 'But I didn't contract to do this all by myself!' Finally the reality of it sank in."

Kay had done weaving before as a hobby, and now she decided to set up a studio in her home and make it her profession. The expense of putting two children in day care was a factor, but Kay had other reasons as well. "I feel that input at an early age is very important," she says. "It's a time when a lot of things are molded."

Kay found her visions of the babies playing happily with bits of colored yarn while she sat at her loom never materialized. The babies' demands often interrupted her work. "Kids don't always behave the way you expect," she says ruefully.

But there were beautiful moments, too. One child learned to spin fleece sitting in her mother's lap when she was only two years old. Anyone who has tried to work a spinning wheel will appreciate that achievement! Now that both girls are five, Kay has made them little cardboard looms, and they sit and work with her. "They are getting an appreciation of craftsmanship," says Kay.

Kay's main trouble has been getting blocks of time to work. At first she relied a lot on nights and nap times. When the children reached nursery-school age she enrolled them in a morning program and was able to teach some weaving classes through adult education and a local shop.

In the afternoons the children are at home with their mother. They have learned to be very understanding when she has deadlines, and play in their rooms or outside. Kay designed her studio with a view of the children's outdoor play area so she can keep an eye on them while she works.

The second problem has not been with the children but with adults. "People don't take you seriously when you work at home," says Kay, adding her complaint to those of many artists who work at home. "We need to educate adults that it is work." In practical terms this means things like getting friends not to call during working hours just to chat.

Kay has taken her children everywhere from show openings to a three-month wool-buying trip to Greece. Their experiences have taught them how to handle themselves in a variety of situations. One girl flew from California to New York alone only two days after her fifth birthday.

Some parents worry that spending too much time with their children will make the children dependent and clingy. Kay found that spending as much time as possible with them has given the girls a foundation that enables them to be independent and outgoing.

Hospital-Unit Manager/Architectural Draftsman

Robin and Jerry Kaufman wanted their baby to be raised at home, but they knew they wouldn't be able to manage on just one salary. They decided a part-time weekend job for Robin would be a good solution, so when Robin found out she was pregnant she checked the job openings at the hospital where she was working as a staff coordinator and found a position as unit manager. The twenty-hour-a-week job, which entitles her to full benefits, entails working 9:00 to 5:00 every weekend and on alternate Mondays. Jerry, an architectural draftsman, asked his employer if he could have alternate Mondays off in return for working nine hours a day. He agreed to waive overtime pay if he could have that schedule, and his employer consented. "I think the fact that my employer is a woman helped her to be understanding." The Kaufmans, both in their thirties, felt comfortable with the thought of Jerry's sharing in the child raising. "Because we were older our decisions were less based on what we were 'supposed to' do."

Robin used all her accumulated vacation and overtime in addition to her eight-week disability leave so that she could stay home for the first four months. After that, the new schedule began. "I didn't know what I was getting into," admits Jerry. "I was already thirty-six. I never felt all that close to kids."

A year and a half later Jerry's reservations have disappeared. "I wouldn't have it any other way. I like having the chance to be the primary person in Max's day. I feel very lucky. It's a wonderful thing to watch him grow."

On weekends Max, now nearly two years old, cheerfully says "bus" and "bye-bye" as Robin leaves for work. Jerry assumes full responsibility for Max and the house, including having dinner ready when Robin gets home. How's the cooking? Robin, smiling, registers a mild complaint. "He always cooks the same things. Meat loaf every weekend." Still, Robin is glad to have dinner ready. "I don't do anything in the evening when I come home after work except play with Max."

The arrangement does have some problems. "I wouldn't work this schedule if I didn't have to," says Robin. "I'd prefer to work five P.M. to one A.M. or six P.M. to two A.M. Then we'd have weekends together. This way Max doesn't get to see us together as a family except evenings." Jerry finds he has trouble getting things done around the house. "Right now I have maybe twenty things around here that need to get done. I get maybe one done a weekend. Errands are about eight times more difficult with Max along. I try to go to a lumber store and he gets into all the bins of nails and things." But if house projects are getting neglected, Max isn't. "I always seem to prefer to pay attention to Max."

The Kaufmans agree the advantages far outweigh the problems. "He feels loved and secure. I think he's going to have good self-esteem. And I think it's very valuable for Max to get an idea of what a man can be," says Robin. "He'll be a better father, and hopefully a good match for some woman out there someday." Jerry adds, "He's a very independent baby, not timid about new experiences."

Robin and Jerry plan to have another child next year, and then continue their present schedule for another five years. Once the children are school-age, Robin looks forward to a weekday work schedule. But for right now, Max is top priority. As Jerry says, "He wants us, and needs us, and *enjoys* us!"

The Child in the Workplace

Technical Recruiter

"I always thought that if I had children I'd want to be able to spend time with my child—at least the first critical months. I had in mind that the first year I'd stay home." But when Linda Scobey, a technical recruiter, found herself pregnant she and her husband, Jim, discussed finances and concluded that two incomes were essential.

"My boss had her little girl at work and it seemed ideal. She asked me, 'What are you going to do?' and offered me the chance to bring my baby to work. I have a high-pressure job; it requires a lot of energy. I wasn't sure it would work out, but as the time got closer I thought there's no harm trying."

Six weeks after Jeffrey was born, Linda was back on the job—with a bassinet by her side. When Jeffrey needed to nurse, Linda simply locked her door. "One advantage of this arrangement is that it allows Jeffrey to have close contact with me. It allows him more interaction with adults than if I were home full time. All the people in the office love the babies and pick them up and toss them around."

Linda's job involves matching electronics-industry professionals with firms that need people to do contract work. Since Linda does interviews for up to three hours a day, after a month and a half the arrangement changed. She and her boss began to share the services of a sitter at work. The arrangement is still very different from the on-site child care being offered by some companies. Linda sees more of her baby and the two children have a person who is just for them. Also, Linda has a say in who that person is. She is able to keep an ear out and be aware of what is going on—something that would be impossible if Jeffrey were in a day care center or even with a sitter at home.

Being able to keep an ear out proved useful. Linda would hear her baby crying in another room and not be sure the sitter was trying to do anything about it. She describes the feeling as "total conflict." The situation improved with a new sitter Linda feels she can trust. Now the babies have an office set up for them, complete with a playpen and a baby swing. The sitter takes the babies out for walks around the complex and to a nearby park. Linda always brings a bag lunch so she will have a full hour with her baby at lunchtime.

Like many mothers, she feels working full time is a compromise. "One job is doing my work and being productive, and one is being a mother to my child." It's almost harder having the baby so close and yet not being able to drop what she is doing and scoop him up in her arms anytime. "It's like being on a diet, and someone over there is eating cheesecake. It takes discipline to focus on the job." But Linda is happy to have Jeffrey close to her. "When you need someone to cheer you up and you look at your baby and he smiles—well, that's a real lift!"

Waitress, Secretary, Janitor, Housecleaner, Baker

Eva Vallas has been separated since her daughter, Rosie, was three months old. Because doctors had told her she could never have another child, Eva resolved to spend as much time with her daughter as possible.

"Raising my child has been top priority to me," she says.

Juggling her responsibilities as a mother and breadwinner was not easy, especially since Rosie was still nursing. Determined to keep her baby close to her, Eva took a job as a cocktail waitress. While she worked the baby slept in a bassinet in the business office. Eva arranged a schedule that allowed her to nurse Rosie during her breaks.

Later she found other jobs she could bring Rosie to. She worked briefly as a secretary in a dean's office ("If it had only been the filing and typing maybe I could have managed, but the phones..."), then as a janitor in a bar ("It was great—I could work my own hours as long as I was done by noon"), as a housecleaner ("The bachelors didn't come on to me since I had a kid!"), and as a baker ("Rosie had a cozy bed in the room where we did the baking").

When Rosie reached kindergarten age, Eva took a job four days a week at a home for disturbed teenage boys, and now that Rosie is entering first grade she has decided to increase it to a full five.

Eva laughs about the paths she has chosen in order to stay with her daughter, saying, "It's not for the status-conscious!"

Not only were her jobs far from prestigious, but there were times between jobs when Eva had to fall back on AFDC. Still, Eva feels it has all been worth it.

"There is nothing more important to me than raising a healthy, well-balanced human being," she says, "and I believe I've done that."

Ceramist

Maxine Donner made ceramics as a hobby. She had not thought of making it her living until seventeen months ago, when a divorce left her with a four-year-old daughter and an eight-year-old son. Maxine considered putting the younger child in a day care center and the older one in an after-school program so she could go to work. After looking around briefly, she decided that that was unacceptable to her.

"I just couldn't do it," she says. Then, remembering the pressures she faced, she adds, "It was hard *not* to do."

Maxine found a job in a ceramics studio and enrolled her daughter in a part-time preschool program. Now she arranges to have both children with her after school. At the studio they make things with clay or play outside. This arrangement is possible partly because Maxine's boss is herself a single mother and knows what it's like.

"She's very understanding," says Maxine. "It sure helps."

Figure Salon Proprietor/Physician

"I always wanted to be at home with my baby. But I feel better if I can go out of the house and get some exercise and talk to people. Then I enjoy him more." Liba Placek has found a way to spend time with her son, Michael, and still earn some money and get the outside stimulation she wants. As owner of the Lean Jean Figure Salon in Pompton Lakes, New Jersey, she was able to phase back into work gradually, starting with one or two hours a week in the first weeks after Michael's birth. Now Michael is three and a half months old and she works twenty to thirty hours a week, teaching a number of classes, including prenatal exercise classes.

In the daytime Michael sometimes stays home with his father, Karel, a physician who is studying for his American medical boards. "It's great fathers can do something mothers can do. I'm comfortable knowing Michael is as happy at home with his father as he is with me," says Liba.

Other times, Liba takes Michael with her to the figure salon. "He enjoys being there. He smiles at everyone, and everyone loves him." Some of the women who attended the prenatal exercise class Liba taught when she herself was pregnant are coming to the figure salon again as new mothers, and they feel a special bond with Liba and Michael. There is a nursery at the figure salon, open from 9:00 A.M. to 3:00 P.M., but Liba doesn't leave Michael there for more than an hour if he is awake.

In the evenings Liba makes sure Michael is bathed and fed early, and she takes him back with her to the figure salon, where she works from 6:00 P.M. to 10:00 P.M. Michael has a cradle at the salon, and he sleeps through these evening classes.

Liba found that putting Michael on a schedule was very important in ensuring his comfort. By getting him used to nursing on a schedule, she is able to leave him with his father, knowing he won't get unhappy as long as she is back within three hours.

As Michael gets older, he will spend a little more time in the nursery at the figure salon. But he won't be there too many hours a day. "I'm an earth-mother type," says Liba, laughing. "I wouldn't want him to be in someone else's care for too long."

If Liba and Karel had not immigrated, Liba would have been entitled to a two-year paid child care leave. Nevertheless, they would rather be in the United States. They are proud of their little son, and happy they have worked out a way to both spend time with him.

Patterns of work and parenting are changing, allowing parents choices that did not exist a few decades ago. As more parents find work alternatives that avoid full-time day care for their own children, they open up new possibilities for other working parents in their place of work. And as more people take advantage of these opportunities, what was once an exception becomes a rule. Many employers are becoming receptive to arrangements that previously were unacceptable. The Freierts had an easier time getting a shared position at Gustavus Adolphus College because another couple, the Deans, had already broken the ice. Now Gustavus Adolphus has four couples on the faculty who share positions. Linda Scobey was able to bring her baby to work because her boss had already chosen that alternative for her own baby and was willing to let Linda go the same route. These "chain reactions" are very important to the process of change in employment options for working parents.

While some parents who choose to work at home are mainly concerned with being able to spend more time with their child, the couples who choose to share child care usually have a personal commitment to changing certain roles or attitudes prevalent in our society. Parents of boys are especially concerned that their sons spend time around their father and see their father in a nurturing role. Almost all households where parents share child care also share cooking and other household chores, which means that the child gets to see Dad cooking, grocery shopping, and pushing a vacuum cleaner while Mom goes off to work, and vice versa. Most parents who have worked out such arrangements believe that this will help the child to be a better father, and a gentler and more compassionate human being.

Most full-time working mothers and a growing number of fathers would be happy to take a paid child care leave if it was available. At present, many mothers go back to work as soon as possible out of financial necessity or because their job would not be held for them, and few employed fathers can take a paternity leave. In spite of these pressures, many parents who have worked full time until the birth of their child have managed to rearrange their lives, sometimes making the transition to part-time work or even full-time child raising. The consensus is that the work and planning are worth it, and the rewards of being a part-time or full-time child raiser more than repay the effort.

Most mothers who work part time consider this an ideal situation as long as they can care for their child while they work, or the child can be in the care of the father. Only a few of the mothers the authors interviewed expressed a strong desire to be a full-time child raiser for five years; most wanted the diversity of a part-time job. However, when the father is working full time and the mother is working part time, a lack of time for family activities and leisure is a problem. The Freierts' arrangement of *both* working part time appeared to be the most successful in terms of satisfying their child's needs while still having a reasonable amount of time together evenings and weekends.

Self-employed parents expressed problems common to all self-employed people, including fluctuations of income, the long period necessary to build up a clientele, and lack of contact with peers. However, they also appreciated the many benefits, especially the flexibility in scheduling their time.

Most parents who work full time consider it a compromise for their child's early years, and while many determined parents are finding solutions to this problem, paddling upstream is not easy. Individual solutions do work for the American family, but parents hope the government and private employers will become increasingly responsive and will create more choices reflecting a growing respect for the needs of the family in contemporary society. Meanwhile, personal solutions show the ingenuity and determination of parents who recognize the importance of their role in nurturing and child raising.

Chapter Fourteen

The Future for the Working Parent: Choices and Changes

The Computer: Redefining the Workplace

Computer technology is already changing the nature of work and the workplace for a growing number of employed and self-employed workers throughout the United States. This technology, along with other interfacing high technologies, challenges our current definitions about a job, and will make alternative work arrangements like part-time work, job sharing, flexiplace, flexitime, and maxiflex increasingly attractive to even the most conservative employers. Economic feasibility and cost-cutting are something that all companies can appreciate, and the prospect of reduced overhead and increased efficiency is something they cannot ignore. An additional attraction is improved worker morale as employees see expanded flexibility and choices in their work life.

Changes favorable to working parents and child raisers from the continued growth of computer technology are accelerating what would otherwise be a rather slow process of change in employers' attitudes toward working parents and their child-raising responsibilities. While it is true that innovations like job sharing and flexitime are already being implemented in many large companies, computers directly enhance the feasibility of these work arrangements by introducing a system where work hours can be logged on terminals located at home or in the workplace, and where computers can be open and ready for business whether it is 9:00 A.M. or midnight. Computers do not get tired and irritable even at 11:00 P.M. after working a twelve-hour day; it's all up to the input of the user.

With her two children—Kevin, one year old, and Timmy, three—safely in bed, Susan Hansberry sits in the family room of her Westford, Massachusetts, home quietly working at the keyboard of her computer terminal. Using an ordinary telephone, Susan's portable terminal instantaneously communicates with its superior, a computer located in Billerica at the office of Honeywell, her employer and one of the country's biggest computer manufacturers.

Susan Hansberry began working for Honeywell part time at home two and a half years ago. Not wanting to combine full-time work and child raising, Susan left her job as administrative secretary at Honeywell before her first child was born. When Timmy was almost one, she was offered the opportunity to work part time at home, and she jumped at the chance. Now she reports to work at the computer terminal in her home.

Susan does text editing of the software release bulletins customers get when they buy a Honeywell computer. She works with a writer at Honeywell, and they "talk" via the terminal or by telephone. A copy of what Susan has entered in her terminal prints out immediately at Honeywell, where the writer can check it over.

The hours are perfect for Susan, and she can work anytime except lunch hour and Thursday nights and holidays, when the computer room is closed. When Timmy was a baby she sometimes worked for short periods with him in the playpen. Now Timmy has a little brother, Kevin, and the days are busy. Susan usually starts work at 8:00 P.M., after the boys have been tucked in for the night. Her husband, an accounting manager, occasionally has to work late into the evening, so she enjoys having work to fill her evening hours.

Occasionally Susan has a rush job, and then she may work on a Saturday and ask her husband to watch the boys, or she may ask Timmy to play by himself for a little while during Kevin's nap. "If you let me finish my work, I'll let you work," she tells him. Timmy's reward for letting his mommy work is to get to type on the terminal himself. "I'm doing my work," he says proudly.

Because Susan is quite experienced, she finds the work does not always demand all her concentration. She can even do it while watching TV. She likes the informality of work at home. "I can do it in pajamas if I want to!"

Across the country, a few companies are experimenting with workers at home using home-based computer terminals, and a number of self-employed professionals are also working at home with their computers, but this is really only the beginning of a computer revolution that will affect all aspects of our daily lives. In the work world, a multifaceted electronic telecommunications network that is capable of continually accepting the input of data from large numbers of workers, and also capable of instantaneously processing and delivering that information to points across the country, will allow a flexibility in work location, working hours, and weekly scheduling that will greatly benefit working parents. In a survey conducted by General Mills, 66 percent of 104 corporations surveyed said that they expected, within the next five years, to have maxiflex programs allowing workers to log seventy hours every two weeks. It is computer technology that will facilitate these kinds of arrangements.

Computer-based job sharing, part-time work, and maxiflex will enable working parents to spend a great deal of time with their children and also maintain a reasonable level of earnings because their time away from the children will be very efficiently converted to work time. Susan Hansberry's hourly wage at her part-time computer-based job would be substantially reduced if she had to pay child care expenses for two children and commute costs. Her working hours can be very early or late, during her children's nap, or on weekends, and work can be interrupted if a child wakes up or suddenly spills the orange juice.

Depending on a child's age and the number of children in the family, a working child raiser could easily log as much as thirty to thirty-five hours per seven-day week just by working during the breaks from child care that naturally occur: nap times, after bedtimes, and the breaks that happen on the weekends as well. A baby can easily nap a total of five hours a day; add one or two hours in the evening after bedtime and this would yield thirty-five work hours per week without even any weekend time.

And the advantages of such a computer-based, flexiplace work force apply to employers and the self-employed as well. As compensation for providing workers with maximum flexibility, employers will find actual number of hours worked remaining high as employees find it easy to log hours. Employer overhead costs will be reduced and work efficiency will be high as sudden inspirations and spurts of work energy will all be logged. And worker morale, including that of working parents, will improve. Parents will enjoy not having to sacrifice their family life for their job.

Futurists like Alvin Toffler predict that by the twenty-first century computer technology will reverse the urbanization spawned by the Industrial Revolution and will create a society of home-based workers. With what he calls the electronic cottage established, workers' ties with their community will be strengthened and centralization and long commutes will be a thing of the past. While crystal balls are always murky, the computer revolution is already beginning to fulfill this prophecy, and the concept of work is being redefined. In the past, centralization and role expectations emphasized the importance of physical presence in the workplace, but computer-based activities redefine work as energy put into the system; physical presence or location is irrelevant to a computer, and a computer doesn't care about the color of your tie.

Looking into the future, working parents have cause for optimism. Aside from computer-based jobs, alternative work arrangements like job sharing and flexitime are being implemented by many employers, and according to the General Mills survey, a majority of corporations plan to adopt a flexitime program and a shorter-workweek option within the next five years. It has been predicted that within ten years 25 percent of the work force will be on flexitime and about 30 percent will be job sharing or working part time.

Trends in Employment

The trend toward part-time work is particularly marked; in the last decade the number of part-time workers has grown three times as fast as the number of full-time workers. While workers have a number of reasons for wanting to work part time, including going to school and phasing into retirement, the majority of part-time workers are women. A 1978 survey by the National Commission on Working Women showed that almost a quarter of women working full time would work part time if work were available, and about half of all women looking for jobs hoped to find part-time work.

Unions are beginning to recognize that some of their members want part-time work, and in the next decade they may become more responsive to this need. A smaller percentage of the work force belongs to unions now than a decade ago. In order for organized labor to remain a powerful force in this country, it will probably begin to court the large number of women who are part-time workers. Currently, fewer than 10 percent of part-time women workers belong to a union. If these women felt their needs were being well represented, their numbers could swell the ranks of the unions.

The unionization of part-time workers would greatly benefit families where both parents want to work and to share child care. At present, many families need to have one parent in the work force full time in order to get medical and other important benefits. As benefits become more standard for part-time employees, it will be more possible for each parent to work less than full time.

Better-paying jobs for women will also assist families who want to share work and parenting. According to Bureau of Labor Statistics, women still earn only 60 percent of male incomes. As a result, when a husband and wife both work half-time, their combined income may not be adequate. This inequity often forces parents into traditional roles when they would prefer alternative arrangements. But the role of women in the workplace is changing. Women are working as journeymen in blue-collar trades and have entered formerly all-male fields, becoming security guards, construction workers, and clergy. In the last ten years the proportion of women judges and lawyers has increased from 4 percent to 14 percent. As women enter better-paying jobs and part-time work becomes available and acceptable, it will be possible for couples to share breadwinning and parenting without putting their children in day care. It will also be possible for single parents to support themselves and their children on a part-time salary.

If a shorter workweek does not become a reality for all workers, it may at least be possible for the self-employed to work part time without invalidating their abilities in their clients' eyes. We are accustomed to not calling our accountant on a Sunday; we could just as easily get used to not bringing the dog to the vet for shots on a Wednesday, and not getting our teeth cleaned on a Friday. We need to remember the five-day workweek is arbitrary, and that while a four-day workweek sounds strange to us, it is not so long ago that our five-day workweek would have been unthinkable.

The current intense pressures of the family versus work and work-related responsibilities will be greatly reduced by the continued growth of work options like job sharing and flexitime. In spite of the recent recession, this process of change in the working world has continued, and so there is every reason to expect that this trend will remain strong, and will become even more rapid if the future is one of renewed economic growth and a reasonable control of inflationary tendencies. At the very least, working parents and parents-to-be have a basis for a cautious optimism when considering the prospects for a balanced and less stressful combination of work and family life.

Family Advocacy

A change in attitude toward parents and children is badly needed. There is still a great deal of prejudice against children, particularly a feeling that different means inferior. But a new movement, reflected by changing legislation and some interesting changes in legal practices, is under way, encouraging a more enlightened attitude toward children and childhood.

The increasing prevalence of job sharing and other work options benefits children as well as their parents, but these changes do not represent a direct recognition of children's needs and rights so much as a response to the needs of working parents. However, the initiation of the federally funded Head Start program—part of the Economic Opportunity Act of 1964—was a very important step. It acknowledged the fact that the early experiences, at least learning experiences, of young children could be crucial to their development. The program also stimulated more interest and research on the importance of early childhood experiences and early childhood education. In addition, more recently there has been an explosion of research and interest in newborn and very young children, with discoveries about the very young child's intellectual abilities and the ability to recognize and relate to specific adults.

Paralleling this development, our legal system is beginning to view children in a new light. In child custody cases, the wishes and perceptions of the child are taken more seriously now than in the past, and children, even preschoolers, are being allowed to testify in cases of child abuse and other serious offenses. While it is only a beginning, these official sanctions cause adults to reevaluate their attitudes toward children, making people feel that children should be taken more seriously.

In order to stimulate change in attitudes toward children and toward child raising, parents must get involved. Working parents who understand the importance of child raising can create more choices for themselves and their families by organizing a family rights movement throughout the United States. There is no reason why the United States must be a backwater; our country has the resources to institute social policy changes to benefit families that would make it a model among industrialized nations. If parents let legislators know their priorities, change can begin to happen.

In 1981 California Assemblyman Art Agnos introduced a bill (AB3770) that would have given all working parents in California—mothers and fathers—the right to take a four-month leave of absence after the birth or adoption of a child. It proposes a shorter leave than many European countries, and it would have been unpaid; but this kind of legislation is a necessary first stage in the movement toward choices for working parents. While the bill failed, Assemblyman Agnos plans to reintroduce it in the future, perhaps in 1984. Such bills need the vigorous support of all parents and future parents.

There are two areas that will dovetail in creating the family advocacy movement in the United States. The first is individual advocacy by parents and other interested individuals. Letters *do* make a difference. When a piece of legislation favorable to working parents is introduced in a state legislature, people in all districts can help its passage by writing to the author of the bill and to their own representatives. The letter should mention the number and author of the bill, explain why it deserves support, and ask the representative's position on the issue. In states where proposed legislation does not yet exist, parents can write their representatives requesting that they author such legislation, showing that support would be forthcoming if such a bill were introduced. Working parents, and workers who know they may someday become parents, are a huge constituency; once they begin to realize their power and let their voice be heard, the cry will be loud enough to echo across the country and reverberate in Washington.

While individual advocacy is important, a second necessary area is political organization. The authors believe that a national organization of working parents is needed. It will be effective in organizing around the issues of concern to working parents—like maternity and paternity leaves, job sharing, parental sick leave, and the right of a father to take off work to attend a birth. The organization's activities would include lobbying, alerting members about pending legislation through a newsletter, and bringing the needs of children and working parents into the public eye. Branch chapters would send speakers to engagements at community meetings and set up booths to distribute information at fairs and conferences. The membership will grow as parents read about the organization in the media, see notices in churches, temples, schools, and libraries, and realize that at last there is an organization that speaks to their needs. Alliances with existing organizations will be helpful. Union members could begin to demand that provisions for parental responsibilities be recognized when a new contract is being negotiated.

There is a great precedent for such movements that begin as grass-roots political organizations and are capable of making a significant impact. For example, Mothers Against Drunk Drivers was started in 1980 in a spare bedroom by Candy Lightner, whose daughter was killed by a drunk driver. Two and a half years later, the organization has 50,000 members and 115 chapters in thirty-five states, and has already had an influence in the passage of stronger penalties for drunk driving. Its membership is not just mothers but all people who care about the tragic alcohol-related loss of human life that takes place on our roads and highways.

Because the day care issue affects the whole society, a family advocacy organization's membership would not be limited to working parents or child raisers, and it would be multi-issue in its approach. Young and as yet unmarried adults, grandparents, teachers, pediatricians, clergy, and others could all join in the fight to give working parents and their children more options.

There are concerned people in all states, all income brackets, all political parties, and all kinds of occupations. All that is needed is the recognition that the passive "parents have no choice" syndrome is a self-fulfilling prophecy. Things *can* get better if people join forces. The beginnings of such a movement for the right of a family to be a family will be followed by an avalanche of support and change that will sweep away the outmoded attitude toward working parents and benefit the whole society.

Some Concluding Thoughts

The day care issue and pressures on contemporary family life raise questions about our society and where we want to be going as a people. The cliché that modern life is increasingly impersonal and dehumanized is nevertheless quite true, and there is an impoverishment of spirituality and brotherhood as materialism and competitiveness continue to be overemphasized. Such an environment is hardly supportive of family life and the goals of family living, and the stresses and strains are evident.

Technology is synonymous with convenience, but it also tends to create distance and barriers—an indirect way of relating to other people and the world. We have lost much of our ability to spontaneously cooperate with each other because there is little in modern life that requires this ability. Recognizing the trend, the commune movement of the sixties reacted against this. Today, many people miss a communal element in their lives. One full-time child raiser who lives in a town of about twenty-five thousand people finds, "[There is] the isolation that is the outcome of a society which places emphasis on privacy, single-family homes, the noncommunal aspects of the way we live and work. I would rather live in a small community that shares certain responsibilities—the garden, the cooking, the baby-sitting, the laundry, and so on."

The feeling of community and family is of great importance, and we should make it a priority. Because there is a basic need to feel that one belongs and to feel that that acceptance is generally acknowledged, alienation is not a neutral experience. Alienation is an enormously harmful force, frequently ending in violence or self-destruction. It is undoubtedly a factor in the tragically skyrocketing child and teenage suicide rates. Only a strengthening of genuine closeness and connectedness in the family and community can reverse this trend.

The industrial and high technology revolutions seem to carry us along toward a predetermined future. This passive feeling and a sense of helplessness are evident in the issue of day care and its role in our fast-changing society: "Day care is here to stay." "It's what's happening. How can we question it?" Indeed it is happening, and we as a society are allowing it to happen, either out of complacency or because we don't realize we have any say or influence.

We can influence the future. What is needed is a new altruism and a realistic, honest humanism. Respect for and belief in the importance of closeness and interpersonal relationships, including the family, which has the natural potential to be a place for closeness and connectedness in our society, is important. A change in traditional roles does not diminish the capacity or need for friendships, love relationships, and family relationships to provide a basic tribal connectedness and feeling of belonging that we all need.

Appendix I

The "Day Care Diseases"

The following is a brief review of some of the important day care–associated infections. It is by no means exhaustive, as there are a great variety of bacteria, viruses, and other infectious agents that are capable of producing disease. This is intended as a guide to inform parents of some of the more common infections responsible for outbreaks or epidemics. It is not intended as medical advice or to be used for self diagnosis. Many different diseases can present the same symptoms. If a child seems seriously ill, prompt medical advice should be sought, and the problem treated if necessary.

Hepatitis type A: It is believed that there are three kinds of hepatitis virus: type A, or infectious hepatitis; type B, or serum hepatitis; and a form known as non-A, non-B. Day care center outbreaks are almost exclusively type A, which has an incubation period of two to six weeks, at which point the individual may suffer from weakness, fever, loss of appetite, abdominal discomfort, headache, and jaundice. Transmission is through fecal-oral contamination. It is estimated that 85 percent of adults recover uneventfully after six to eight weeks and almost all others within four months. A small percentage of cases develop into a life-threatening disease or result in complications. Pregnant women, diabetics, and the elderly are high-risk groups and may need hospitalization. There is a serious problem of early detection in day care centers because preschool age children generally have mild nonspecific symptoms, or no symptoms at all. Outbreaks pose a threat to the community, with disease spreading to parents, day care workers, and other people. Various laboratory tests including a test for presence of antibodies, indicating infection, are available. Dr. Stephen Hadler of the Centers for Disease Control has found that the spread of hepatitis in day care centers can be limited by an organized program of injections of immunoglobulin given to all exposed center children and employees. Immunoglobulin can prevent infection or increase the body's resistance to the virus and it is effective for several months. Illness can be prevented if globulin is given within one to two weeks of exposure. Once infection occurs, there is no specific treatment for the disease and it must run its course. Preventive vaccine is not currently available.

Bacillary dysentery (shigellosis): This is usually a serious and highly contagious bacterial disease in children, particularly under two years. Infected adults may have slightly milder symptoms. Stool cultures are usually a reliable test. Live bacteria are present in stools. Latent infections can occur. Transmission is, like hepatitis, fecal-oral. In young children the typical picture is an abrupt appearance of fever, chills, cramps, and diarrhea. There may be a fever as high as 104°F. Blood and mucus may be seen in the stools. In very young children hospitalization is often necessary, with careful monitoring. Debilitated patients are a high-risk group and may get secondary infections due to other organisms. Children or adults with chronic incurable intestinal diseases like ulcerative colitis and Crohn's disease may be very hard hit. Ampicillin is usually used to combat the bacteria that has invaded the intestinal tract. However, some strains are resistant to ampicillin, and in this case trimethoprimsulfamethoxazole (Septra, Bactrim) may be used. Treatment is also aimed at controlling symptoms and at restoring acid-base imbalances and correcting dehydration. Dehydration is a serious threat to infants and must be treated promptly. With prompt treatment, the prognosis is good except in very young infants, to whom the disease is life-threatening. Infection does not result in lifelong immunity and reinfection can occur. There is no specific prevention for this disease. Children may be contagious for weeks after symptoms have subsided.

Giardiasis: This intestinal infection is caused by a protozoa called *Giardia lamblia.* It can usually be detected by stool samples or intestinal biopsy. Symptoms are usually mild, with slowly developing diarrhea. Untreated infections may persist for months, with diarrhea, weight loss, and abdominal discomfort, and occasionally more severe symptoms. Many cases are asymptomatic. Metronidazole (Flagyl) is the drug of choice, but has recently been shown to be carcinogenic in animals. There is no specific prevention, but prognosis is excellent. Reinfection can occur.

Hemophilus influenzae type B: This bacteria is capable of causing a number of diseases, depending on the location of the infection in the body, and typically attacks children four months to five years of age. After the neonatal period it is the major cause of childhood bacterial meningitis. Asymptomatic infections of the nose and throat may occur. Infants with an invasive infection of the brain or spinal cord (meningitis) usually have fever, weakness, and a high-pitched cry. The bacteria may also infect other areas simultaneously, and is usually present in the blood (bacteremia). The fontanel may be tight or bulging. Cultures must be taken from the blood or cerebrospinal fluid to confirm the diagnosis, and examination of other bodily fluids or secretions may be helpful. Treatment consists of hospitalization with intravenous antibiotics to combat the life-threatening infection. Supportive therapy with oxygen and tube feedings may be necessary. The danger is greatest for very young infants. Overall, 5 to 10 percent of young children will not survive the infection.

In addition to meningitis, *Hemophilus* can also attack the joints, skin and underlying tissues (cellulitis), middle ear (acute otitis media), epiglottis, lungs, and sac surrounding the heart (pericardium). With the exception of an ear infection, all of these diseases usually require hospitalization. An inflammation of the epiglottis (epiglottitis) can be dangerous, as the airway can become obstructed. Prompt insertion of a tube to ensure adequate air supply is critical. All of these diseases are treated with appropriate antibiotics and other supportive measures. With ampicillin-resistant strains of the bacteria, chloramphenicol may be used, but should be carefully monitored in very young infants because of an occasional toxic reaction. Most children will recover completely. No specific prevention or vaccine is available. Between the ages of four and eight children develop antibodies that make later invasive infections less likely.

Appendix II

National Job Sharing Network Members

Arizona
 Work Life Options
 1202 E. Maryland, Suite 2H
 Phoenix, AZ 85014

California
 Flexible Career Associates
 P.O. Box 6701
 Santa Barbara, CA 93111

 New Ways to Work
 149 Ninth Street
 San Francisco, CA 94103

Colorado
 Innovative Career Options
 University of Denver
 Cooperative Education Program
 University Park
 Denver, CO 80204

Connecticut
 Family and Career Together
 1007 Farmington Ave., Suite 15
 West Hartford, CT 06107

Georgia
 Part-time Work Options
 c/o Muffie Michaelson
 28 Roanoke Avenue, N.E.
 Atlanta, GA 30305

Iowa
 Project Job Share
 Division of Women's Programs
 Drake University
 2700 University Avenue
 Des Moines, IA 50311

Maine
 Nancy Viehmann
 Pier Road, Box 78
 Cape Porpoise, ME 04014

Massachusetts
 Work Options Unlimited
 645 Boylston Street
 Boston, MA 02116

Minnesota
CHART, Job Sharing Project
Wesley Temple Building
123 E. Grant Street
Minneapolis, MN 55403

New Jersey
Adult Career Exploration Center
Counseling Center, Memorial Hall
Glassboro State College
Glassboro, NJ 08028

New York
Workshare
311 E. 50th Street
New York, NY 10022

Oregon
Flexible Ways to Work
c/o YWCA
1111 S.W. Tenth Avenue
Portland, OR 97205

Pennsylvania
Center for Flexible Employment
3060 Bristol Road
P.O. Box 404
Bensalem, PA 19020

Job Partner Service of the
  Job Advisory Service
300 S. Craig Street
Pittsburgh, PA 15213

Work Time Options
966 Summer Place
Pittsburgh, PA 15243

Texas
Women's Employment Advocacy
  Program
Austin Women's Center
1505 W. 6th Street
Austin, TX 78702

Utah
Phoenix Institute
383 South 600 East
Salt Lake City, UT 84102

Virginia
Association of Part-time
  Professionals
P.O. Box 3632
Alexandria, VA 22302

Washington
FOCUS
509 10th Avenue East
Seattle, WA 98102

Suggested Reading

Books

Fraiberg, Selma. *Every Child's Birthright: In Defense of Mothering.* New York: Basic Books, 1977.

———. *The Magic Years.* New York: Charles Scribner's Sons, 1968.

Glickman, Beatrice Marden, and Springer, Nesha Bass. *Who Cares for the Baby?: Choices in Child Care.* New York: Schocken Books, 1978.

Levine, James. *Who Will Raise the Children?: New Options for Fathers and Mothers.* Philadelphia: J. B. Lippincott, 1976.

Spock, Benjamin. *Raising Children in a Difficult Time.* New York: W. W. Norton & Co., 1974.

White, Burton L. *The First Three Years of Life,* Englewood Cliffs, N.J.: Prentice-Hall, 1975.

Newsletters

National Council for Alternative Work Patterns Newsletter. Published by the National Council for Alternative Work Patterns, Inc., 1925 K Street, N.W., Suite 308A, Washington, DC 20006.

New Ways to Work Newsletter. Published by New Ways to Work, 149 Ninth Street, San Francisco, California 94103.

Work Times. Published by New Ways to Work. See above. (An international information exchange on alternative work time.)

The Center for Parent Education Newsletter. Published by The Center for Parent Education, 55 Chapel Street, Newton, Massachusetts 02160.

Index

Abuse, child, 26, 30-31
Adaptation, 83
After school care, 94
Aggressiveness, 26-27
Agnos, Art, 177
Ainsworth, Mary, 36
Association of Part-Time Professionals, 150
AT&T, 153
Attachment, 19-21, 24-26
Attachment and Loss, 37
Austria, 143, 144-145

Baby-sitters, 25, 29-30, 93
Bacillary dysentery, 77, 181
Belsky, Jay, 34, 37
Bettelheim, Bruno, 89
Blanchard, Marie, 61
Bonding, 19, 20-21, 23-24
Boredom (child raisers), 124-127
Bowlby, John, 37
Brazelton, Berry, 30
Breast feeding, 75
Bry, Adelaide, 102

"Cafeteria benefits," 152
California, 150, 152, 154, 177

Carey, Hugh, 150
Centers for Disease Control, 70, 71, 72, 77, 78
Chicago Study of Child Care and Development, 86
Chicken pox, 74
Child abuse, 26, 30-31
Child care leaves, 138-139, 142, 154
  Europe, 138, 140, 142-147
Child custody, 176
Child-support payments, 145
Clarke-Stewart, Alison, 86
Cochran, Moncrieff, 36, 87
Computers
  and work schedules, 171-174
Constancy (attachment), 20-21, 22
Corsini, David, 36
Costs of child care, 132, 140-141
Creativity, 89-90
Cytomegalovirus, 69-70
Czechoslovakia, 22, 140, 143

Daycare, 86
"Day Care Can Be Dangerous," 39
Day care centers, 26-27, 28
  See also Diseases; Staff
Dehydration, 77
Denmark, 29, 143, 147

187

Determinants of Infant Behavior, 36
Diseases (day care centers), 68-80
Divorce, 30, 53, 145
Doyle, Anna Beth, 72
Dreams, 35
Dysentery, 77, 81

Economic Opportunity Act, 176
Editors, 43, 110
Education, early, 85-91, 116-117
"Effects of Day Care: A Critical Review," 34
Emotional development (infants and toddlers), 19-20
England, 82, 143
Equal Rights for Fathers, 153
Erhardt, Werner, 102
Erikson, Erik, 89
EST, 100
EST: 60 Hours That Transform Your Life, 102
E.T., 65
Every Child's Birthright, 20
Expectations, parental, 55, 88

Family advocacy, 176-178
Family Circle, 33, 42, 76
Farran, Dale, 35
Fathers, 98-100, 121-122, 138, 144, 153-154
First Three Years of Life, 20
Flexitime, 94, 147, 148-149, 150-151, 174
Flowers for Algernon, 65
Ford Foundation, 153
Foster homes, 21-22, 31
Fowler, William, 86
Fraiberg, Selma, 20, 21
France, 138, 143, 144, 145, 146, 147
Freud, Sigmund, 37, 64, 89
Friedan, Betty, 108
Froebel, Friedrich, 82
Frost, Robert, 84

Germany, 82, 138, 143, 144-145, 146
Giardiasis, 182
Guilt issue, 42
Gustavus Adolphus College, 157, 169

Hadler, Stephen, 70, 71, 72, 181
"Hard" data, 35
Hedonism, new, 100, 103, 104
Hemophilus influenzae, 70, 75, 182
Hepatitis, 71-72, 75, 78, 80, 180-181
Herpes simplex, 74
Housewives, status of, 106-112
Hungary, 142, 143

Immune system, 74, 75
Independence, 25, 101, 102-103, 117
Infant centers, 27, 28
Infants in Institutions, 21
Insurance, child care leave, 141
Intelligence, development of, 84
International Symposium on Day-Care Associated Infections, 72
Intimacy, 100-101
Israel, 89
Italy, 143, 144, 146

Job sharing, 148-150, 183-184
Jobs, stresses of, 112, 133

Kagan, Jerome, 39
Katz, Gregor, 144
Kennell, John, 23
Kentucky, 151-152
Khan, Nasim, 86
Kibbutz children, 89
Kindergarten, 82-83, 92
Klaus, Marshall, 23

Levenstein, Phyllis, 24, 87, 88

Index 189

Licensing (day care), 28-29
Lipton, Rose, 21
Loneliness (housewives), 122-123
Looking Out for No. 1, 103

Main, Mary, 61
Maternal deprivation, 21-22
Maternity leaves, 143
　Europe, 138, 140
　See also Child care leaves
Maxiflex, 151, 173
McLuhan, Marshall, 42
Measles, 74
Media, mass, 42-43, 114
Meningitis, 70-71
Moskowitz, Debbie, 36
Mother-Child Home Program, 87
Mothers Against Drunk Drivers, 178
Multiple sclerosis, 74
Musical skills, 48-49

Nannies, 25, 29-30, 93
New York City Infant Day Care Study, 87
Nolte, Judith, 110
Nursery schools, 26, 81-82
Nursing-time allowance, 146
Nurturing, 20

Of Mice and Men, 65
Orff, Carl, 48
Orphans, 21-22
Ostracism, 90
Owen, Robert, 81

Parent-Infant Bonding, 23
Parental expectations, 55, 88
Parental sick leave, 79, 139, 142, 146-147, 152
Part-time work, 112, 149-150, 174-175

Pass, Robert F., 69
Paternity leaves, 98-99, 153
Perl, Fritz, 103
Phoenix, 71
Portnoy, Fern, 36
Prejudice (against children), 64-65
Preschools, 82-83, 84-85
　See also Kindergarten; Nursery schools
Procter & Gamble, 153
Project Head Start, 82, 176
Provence, Sally, 21
Psychoanalytic studies, 37

Raising Children in a Difficult Time, 20, 89, 108
Ramey, Craig, 35
Reentry (to workforce), 133-134
Researchers, 38-40
Ricciuti, Henry, 36
Ringer, Robert, 103, 104
Role models, 90

Scarf, Maggie, 112
Schuman, Stanley, 79
Schwarz, J. Conrad, 36
Second Stage, 108
Separation
　number of hours of, 18, 22, 34, 92-93
　tolerance for, 19
Separation anxiety, 36
Shigellosis, 77, 78, 181
Shingles, 74
Sick leave. *See* Parental sick leave
Simmons, Carolyn, 36
Social-parasite issue, 140
Social Security Act, 141
"Soft data," 35
Soviet Union, 89, 112, 140, 143, 145, 146
Spain, 142, 143, 144, 146
Specificity (attachment), 20-21, 22

Spitz, Rene, 21
Spock, Benjamin, 20, 89, 108
Staff (day care centers), 27, 28, 40-41, 49-50, 62, 79
Steinberg, Laurence, 34, 37
"Strange situation" experiment, 36
Stress, job-related, 112, 133
"Superwoman," 42, 43, 113-114
Sweden, 138, 139, 143, 144, 145, 147

Teachers, parents as, 85-91, 116-117
Toffler, Alvin, 174
Toys, 84
Trust, 20

Unconscious, 37
Unfinished Business: Pressure Points in the Lives of Women, 112
Unions, 151, 174-175

United Kingdom, 143
University of California in Los Angeles, 152
USSR. *See* Soviet Union

Vaccination, 73-74
Vocabularies, 47

West Germany. *See* Germany
Whitbread, Jane, 42
White, Burton, 20, 22
White House Conference on Families, 148
Wittig, Barbara, 36
Women's liberation, 106-108
Women's World, 32
Workplace
 babies at, 166-169